Unscrambling Emails

Preeti Shirodkar

SHROFF PUBLISHERS & DISTRIBUTORS PVT. LTD.
Mumbai Bangalore Kolkata NewDelhi

Unscrambling Emails

by Preeti Shirodkar

First Edition: June 2013

First Reprint: March 2014

ISBN : 978-93-5110-144-4

Published by **Shroff Publishers & Distributors Pvt. Ltd.** C-103, T.T.C. Industrial Area, M.I.D.C., Pawane, Navi Mumbai - 400 705. Tel.: (91-22) 4158 4158 Fax: (91-22) 4158 4141 E-mail: spdorders@shroffpublishers.com. Printed at Repro India Ltd. Mahape Navi Mumbai.

Unscrambling Emails

Preeti Shirodkar

TABLE OF CONTENTS

Foreword

The digital world has over the last century opened up ever greater opportunities and possibilities in numerous spheres; but for the unsuspecting or untrained, it can be a space that is so challenging and overwhelming that one can completely get lost in it and would thus rather avoid it than attempt to benefit from what it has to offer. It is possibly this challenge that books like XXXX for Dummies, a whole series that has tried to train people, who are too shy to ask, unaware of where to get the training or too scared to experiment, seeks to address.

Having crossed all these obstacles myself and realising the need for an easy reference book, to make the most of what emails have to offer, by way of mode of correspondence, I ventured to pen this book. No doubt, emails are in use and abundantly so, yet for most, they are either fun, and a means of staying in touch with friends, or just a basic tool, where most of the interesting features lie unexplored.

My love for words and the desire to surge ahead, with greater grit, the bigger the challenge – traits instilled and nurtured in me by my parents and paternal grandmother – made this a task worth undertaking. The fear of the web world too was not unknown to me, having experienced it myself, seen it in my father, who was otherwise always open to new learning experiences and my colleagues as well as students, who were often struggling with it, but few of whom had the humility or courage to ask and learn.

For the conquest of my fear, I would also like to thank a friend – Rishav Sinha, whom I was introduced to by chance and who opened up for me the treasures of the facilities associated with the email, like google docs and blogs. Yet, despite the knowledge and awareness of the need for such a book, the task of writing it would have gained phantasmagoric dimensions, but for the rock solid support of a team member - Minouti Naik - who doubles up as a shadow, a researcher, a typist and anything I wish her to be. My students have always, in fact, been more than an inspiration – at times challenging me to think of news ways to get across to them, while at others proving to be a solid sense of support, enthusing me and offering me help as I attempt to effectively multitask – one among whom is Priyanka Pengonda, who assisted me in all my primary research for the book, since my Research Associate had just left.

Finally, no task is interesting unless one has solid sound boards – Ameya and Abhishek, a couple of my former students with whom I run the ideas and always get suggestions - and has challenges that make the task more daunting and therefore the desire more insistent, for which I can thank the organisation, I work for.

I hope this journey would prove to be as interesting and enriching for my readers, as it has been for me, for only then would my efforts have been truly rewarded.

Preeti Shirodkar

Evolution of the Email

Over the years, what one cannot deny is either the growing dependence upon the email or its rising popularity. Whether one prefers it or not, and likes it or not, what one cannot deny is that email communication is here to stay.

History

First used in the second half of the 20th century, though by very few people, email has more than half a century of existence. Yet in its early stages not merely was its accessibility restricted, but it was also a charged service. However, with the growing spread and reliance on the computer, popularity of the email as a mode of communication spread, as it was found efficient and fast; and with a growing number of service providers entering the fray, not only did it become free, but also began to boast of increasing number of facilities and features.

Today, email is considered to be the chief form of official communication - both within the organisation and among organisations.

It is believed that today there are more than 2 billion email users and the popularity has grown to such an extent that it is becoming one of the chief forms of reaching out to people, so much so that arguably more than 60% of the emails received everyday are considered non-essential i.e. going beyond the useful.

In fact, the growing dependence upon the email is so high that today we have people across the age groups, from five to a hundred, and only getting younger, as well as people from all across the globe increasingly relying upon it, thereby contributing to its popularity.

Rising dependence on the email

In order to use email effectively, it is important to understand that though it has a very short history, in comparison with other forms of written communication, it is 'the' written communication mode of the present and future, since it offers convenience, speed, cost effectiveness and ease in storage and yet the legal security that goes with the written word. So too, accessibility to the email is on the rise, with internet accessibility through hand held devices, like the tablet and the mobile phone.

And so, while it is a constantly evolving form, being in the nascent stages, when compared to other written modes of communication, it needs to be used in an appropriate manner, both in order for it to be effective and so as to derive maximum benefit from it.

Moreover, it is prone to extreme variation, since it not merely changes with technological development and the resulting innovations, but has users across the globe, who belong to diverse age groups, making the variation extreme. This makes being aware of the medium, the facilities and the challenges extremely vital, if one wants to make it work for oneself, rather than getting caught either in miscommunication or using it as a basic medium to get one's message across.

Email as a convenient replacement of the letter

When one thinks of the email, it is important to remember that it essentially serves as a convenient replacement for the letter, in the context of time taken for delivery, cost, maintaining confidentiality and storage. Moreover, it also affords the legal security and accountability of the written word and has therefore become an increasingly popular and used form of personal and professional written communication. In fact, this transition from letters to emails is so complete that often emails get referred to only as mails, since the former as a means of formal communication have been relegated to the background and actually seem to be bordering on extinction, as an official vehicle of written communication.

Email, instant messaging and chat

The email too has further evolved, not merely in the context of offering more features, but also to serve the requirement of the users, who need a source of instant communication, on the one hand, and have extremely reduced attention spans on the other. Thus while within the context of the email itself one can see the more informal features of chat and hangouts that allow one to communicate in writing in real time, one also needs to credit it with being the chief inspiration in the development of instant messaging that has become an extremely important form of personal as well as professional mode of written communication. Done essentially through brief messages sent using mobile phones/tablets for free, on a pre-subscribed data plan, instant messaging that takes many forms today is, as the very name suggests, a mode of written communication that is immediate in its delivery and access. It is being increasingly used, both in official and personal circles, for sending not merely text matter but also photographs.

Email or e-mail

Often there is a great debate about whether it is more appropriate to use email or e-mail (with or without a hyphen) and though there are avowed followers of both - neither is deemed totally correct or incorrect, as a result of which both are in use. While the argument in favour of the use of e-mail is that it serves to denote that the word in fact is a combination of two words – electronic and mail, thereby necessitating the hyphen, those of the other camp argue that it is more convenient to use it without a hyphen and that with language evolution, there is an attempt to drop the hyphen from a lot of words, in which it was used earlier, for example 'coordinate'. One can therefore use either and be technically correct; however, it is important to maintain consistency in the spelling used and also follow protocol that may be related to the organisation one works for, i.e. while the media prefers e-mail most online matter uses email.

As a popular saying goes, if you cannot beat them join them. And so, in the context of the email, all that the wise would say (and of course do) is perfect the art of using emails as a mode of communication, not merely because it is fast and effective, but more importantly achieving proficiency in this art would not only help one stay ahead in the world of professional competition and personal popularity, but also would make one its master, rather than its slave.

Importance of an email

In its early stages of evolution, in fact even as late as the early 21st century in India, emails could have been considered as a fad and dismissed, since computers were not widely and easily available and accessible. Only the top authorities in an organisation would often have access to a desktop; else there would be a centralised facility for computer access and this would be restricted to some primary functions like computation and at the most record maintenance. Moreover, the access to the web was restricted - both due to its pricing and quality of service. However, with the advent of the 21st century, most of these issues have been taken care of. In this light, emails have become a common and important form of official communication, for a variety of reasons:

- **Free communication**: Except for the internet cost incurred, which too has consistently reduced over time, and a little that may get spent on electricity, to charge the desktop/laptop, emails are totally free. This makes them cost efficient for the organisation/individual.

- **Convenience**: An email can be accessed from anywhere, at any time, even using one's mobile phone, if it has an internet access. This makes it highly convenient. Moreover, documents of a large size can be sent as attachments, while all important accompanying papers can be sent either by scanning them as an image or taking a snapshot. This makes it convenient, both for the sender, who can send it to multiple people or can re-send it at a later point, if need be, and the receiver, who can access it at his/her convenience. Moreover, in a global work culture issues that arise from variations in time zones automatically get resolved, by the use of email.

- **Speed**: Since the email is delivered immediately on sending, delay of any sort, which is bound to occur, even with a courier, let alone a postal delivery, is prevented. This helps in addressing the issues of deadlines and immediacy.

- **Economical**: Since the only real expenses, as mentioned earlier, are those of power consumption and internet accessibility, emails serve as a very economically sound form of communication. Moreover, since they can be sent to multiple receivers at the same time, it further saves cost of paperwork and its movement between people/offices.

- **Security**: Unlike letters and faxed documents that may be misused, if they are left lying around, making them easily accessible to people, emails are more secure, since their accessibility is restricted to the sender and receiver(s). However, it is important to be net savvy and use in-built safety nets that are provided by internet/cyber security laws, like not sharing one's password or keeping it complex. In addition, it is important not to leave one's mailbox open (remaining logged into one's account, when one is not using it), since this makes hacking easy. Despite all this however, no one can completely prevent hacking or ensure 100% security. It is therefore important to understand that email security is not flawless, but if one follows the protocol, it can prove safer than many other forms of communication.

- **Keep a record of the transactions**: In a lot of official communication, it is important for the receiver or sender or both to have a record of the exchange, to minimise legal hassles. This is easily possible in emails, as they can be saved and/or archived. Thus, while offering the comfort of keeping the records, it saves the inconvenience of a large storage space to maintain them. Moreover, it is easy to retrieve them, given the search options made available by the service providers, to enhance their worth. So, although print-outs of emails are possible, they should be stored as soft copies, saving space and paper, while offering the security of possessing a written record.

- **Wide reach**: At a time, one can send an email to as many people as one wishes to, thus saving on one's time and energy; while also reaching out to numerous people, which might help business needs, by providing the scope to reach out to/create a large clientele. Furthermore, it offers the scope to create a group(s), so that one can save time and need not spend it in feeding/selecting the numerous email ids of people, if the receivers are part of the same team, department or office, in the professional space, and family/friends circle in the personal space.

- **Auto-responder**: An email also offers the opportunity for an auto generated out of office response, to indicate to the sender that you would not be able to access your email, until a certain date, so that no misunderstanding results. So too, one can have a fixed sign off saving time, by generating it automatically, rather than feeding it in on every single occasion.

- **Monitoring and managing your business, even if you are not in the office**: Since emails can be accessed from any place, if one has an internet access, on a mobile phone/laptop/desktop, it is easy to constantly monitor professional activities, without necessarily having to be at one's workplace.

- **Reduction of hierarchy, while maintaining its sanctity**: A lot of productive functional time of an office goes in maintaining the protocol, especially in the case of upward communication. This takes away a lot of working hours that could be used to engage in other tasks, in organising and managing things. However, if this is not done, people in authority may look upon it as a violation of protocol. In an email, the various steps in the hierarchical structure can be subverted, by sending out an email, provided one follows the etiquette and protocol that go with the usage of this writing format.

- **A rapid rise in productivity and reduction in expenses**: Since one can manage one's work without being in office and can do so at all times, this helps in significantly reducing wastage of time, thereby increasing productivity. Also, a lot of expenses that would have been incurred, in printing and postage, as well as the costs that would go with the time lag in delivery, automatically get resolved, proving to be doubly beneficial for professionals.

- **Emails are also a great storage for your contacts**: Email accounts are an excellent place to store all contact details of colleagues, clients, potential customers, family, friends, employees and people you used to work together with. This also becomes a source you can access from any place, at any time and can search easily from your database, without having to flip through too many cards. Moreover, they can be as easily edited, making it simple to keep one's contact list up-to-date.

- **Source for professional interaction**: Since emails are flexible, convenient, not particularly time consuming, do not have a long list of to dos with them (like a letter, which needs to be put in an envelope, which in turn needs a stamp affixed, and the letter posted) and do not cost much, among other things, they become an easy means of professional interaction and networking, even if it is to get a feedback on some important concern.

- **Source of getting alerts/reminders etc.:** Most email service providers have the option of the inbox serving as a space for receiving alerts on invitations, events and documents that one may share with a colleague or even birthday reminders, so that one does not miss out on them. This also makes remembering these easy, without putting an additional strain on oneself.

- **Emails are a useful way of reaching out:** For businesses, who advertise online, emails serve as a useful way of getting potential customers. Online advertising and reaching clients/potential customers via email is an inexpensive, immediate and effective way of touching base with or expanding your clientele. So also, some email service providers provide the scope of advertising on their service (email account space). As a result of this, anyone, who uses an email account of that service provider, automatically sees the advertisement. This kind of advertising no doubt comes with a cost, but often this cost is much less than traditional means of advertising like hoardings or television; and though what one can advertise on emails and how one can do it has its own limitations, one cannot deny its wide reach.

This is however not to say that an email is a foolproof way of communication, as due to technological issues the receiver may not actually get the email – it may bounce, go into spam or may get lost in the virtual world. So too, the receiver may deny having received it, although currently service providers do offer solutions like receipt on delivery and receipt on reading. However, the latter still remains in the hands of the receiver, who can choose whether or not to send the receipt on reading. So too, given that uninterrupted power supply and illiteracy are in themselves problems in large parts of the world, to say nothing of computer availability and literacy, emails bring with them their own restrictions and challenges.

Form and Content of an email

The effectiveness of an email would be dependent, at a basic level, on how effectively one is able to make use of the email format. This is because if one is not careful with the format, one might not only land up engaging in miscommunication, but also waste both one's time and that of the other(s), who is the recipient(s) of the email. The email format has two aspects – form and content; and, while the former is made available in a pre-structured manner by the email service provider, constitution of the latter is entirely left to the sender of the email.

Format of the form

The form, the structure of which is provided/designed by the service provider, constitutes the peripheral, but immensely important, elements of an email; these include To, Cc, Bcc and Subject. Using these elements improperly would result in the email not getting the desired value or not evoking the relevant action.

To:

The email ids of all those to whom the mail is to be addressed to are to be included in 'To:'. The 'To:' should include the email ids of all those, who are to act upon the email or are responsible, in the context of the issue under consideration. Care needs to be taken that these are in the descending order of importance – i.e. the senior most person, who is to act upon the mail, is to be addressed first, with others following; the seniority is to be decided however with reference to the content of the email – i.e. who is most concerned with the content.

So too, one can, especially in emails that expect action, mark as 'To:' all those who are accountable for an issue. For example, if one is preparing a report and needs information from specific persons from varied departments, who would have the information, one needs to include them in 'To:'.

Cc:

'Cc:', referring to carbon copy, should include the email ids of all those whom one wants to inform about the content of the mail, but are nevertheless not expected to act upon it; i.e. the content of the email is for their information only. Additionally, the 'Cc:' is also at times used to escalate the matter, if the person(s) marked in 'To:' have not been acting upon the matter. Here too, the names appear in the descending order of seniority.

In case one has included in 'To:' all those who are accountable, one needs to mark as 'Cc:', all those who are responsible. These may include the Heads of those Departments and the individual one is reporting to.

Bcc:

'Bcc:', referring to blank carbon copy, should include the email ids of all those whom one wants to inform about the content of the mail, but without the knowledge of the others, who are included in the 'To:' and 'Cc:'. This would include people like your team members, whom you want to keep in the loop, but who are not directly concerned with the email – by way of action. Moreover, if the others were to know that these people have been kept in the loop, they might take objections/get offended.

One should understand that the reply sent by either the person(s) marked in the Bcc: or Cc: or To: does not reach anyone other than the original sender of the mail, unless one presses the 'reply all' button. Even then, the reply sent by those marked in To: or Cc: will not reach the person included in the Bcc:, although the 'reply all' button is hit.

Suggestions for whom to send:

If one often sends emails to certain groups of people, whether they are one's colleagues, family members or friends, as per the service provider, either the entire list appears, when one types the first email id from the group and one can delete the unwanted recipients from that, else a list of suggestions appears, with 'add' and the person(s) email ids, on clicking on the name that appears, if one wants to include the person(s) suggested.

Subject:

The subject needs to be concise and precise, in order to be effective. It is always better to begin with the word denoting the action expected, followed by the area in which one expects the action to be taken. For example, 'Application for the post of Senior Accounts Manager' or 'Request for zero dialling facility'.

Furthermore, if one is forwarding an email, the word 'Forward' needs to be removed and the subject edited; otherwise the email loses it importance and can confuse the recipient about the expected course of action. Most often forwards are looked upon as the free time actions of the non-serious, especially in official contexts; therefore it is necessary to edit the subject, in order to reflect the true reason for one's forwarding it.

Format of the Content

The content is basically why one sends an email. As a result, the entire framing of the content is dependent upon the sender, especially since there are no indicators for its constitution. While the matter in the content (i.e. the content itself) is totally left to the sender, it is important to follow certain protocol, as regards its structuring, the linguistic aspect and the organisation/ordering of content.

While structuring of the email content has been explained in detail below and the organisation of content has been detailed in Chapter Seven, as regards its linguistic efficiency, care needs to be taken in spelling, grammar and the choice of vocabulary. While one can use external aids – spell check and grammar check - for the first two aspects, one's choice of vocabulary should entirely be based upon an understanding of the audience.

Primarily, one should essentially be aware of one's lacunae in expression, if any, so that one can either choose to call instead of sending ambiguous emails that cannot be understood by the receiver, who has to then anyway call you back for explanation, or, more importantly, one can get basic drafts of the content one needs to send created by someone proficient in communication and then saved as templates, so that they can be used as a part of one's email communication. This is possible because maximum of the work that most people do in an organisation is routine and fairly repetitive, for which templates can help serve the purpose. For example, people who belong to the graphic designing and related areas as well as those who have niche expertise may not be fluent in communication, but may be excellent at their work; such individuals can derive immense benefit by relying on this method.

Salutation

The salutation used would depend upon the company one works for and the receiver(s) at whom the email is targeted. An email may be addressed to an individual or a group of individuals.

The various commonly used forms of salutation are:

- ***Dear Sir***: An extremely formal phrase used to address a gentleman, who is in a position of authority, in a senior position, at your own level, unknown to you or one with whom you share a highly formal official relationship.
- ***Dear Madam***: An extremely formal phrase used to address a lady, who is in a position of authority, in a senior position, at your own level, unknown to you or one with whom you share a highly formal official relationship.
- ***Dear Sir/Madam***: Used if one does not know or is unsure, if the person to whom one is addressing an email is a gentleman or a lady. It is an extremely formal phrase for a person in a position of authority, in a senior position, at your own level, unknown to you or one with whom you share a highly formal official relationship

- ***Dear Mr./Ms. Surname***: Used by most European and Asian companies as a semiformal mode of address for a person with whom one shares an official relationship. Depending upon the organisational culture, it may be used to address one's seniors, juniors or those at the same level as oneself.

- ***Dear Mr./Ms. First Name***: Used by most American companies as a semiformal mode of address for a person with whom one shares an official relationship. Depending upon the organisational culture, it may be used to address one's seniors, juniors or those at the same level as oneself.

- ***Dear First Name***: A semi formal mode of address (but less so) used by most professionals to address colleagues with whom one shares a good rapport

- ***Dear Title (Dr./Prof. et al)***: One could use the title of the person as a form of salutation. This is both formal and conveys deep respect for the person to whom the email is sent.

- ***Dear Colleagues***: When an email is being addressed to many individuals, working for the same organisation, whether senior, junior or at the same level as oneself, one needs to use the term colleagues, to refer to them. Though most believe that colleagues cannot be used for one's seniors, this belief is incorrect as 'colleague' simply means 'a person you work with, especially in a profession or a business'.

Moreover, it is important to note that the English language does not have a phrase like 'Dear All'; therefore, though used rampantly, it is linguistically incorrect.

- ***Dear Team Members***: When an email is being addressed to many individuals, working for the same team, one could use the more intimate 'team members' instead of 'colleagues', essentially if one is the group leader.

  It is also important to note that 'Respected.....' is an outdated mode of address, even in a letter, let alone an email; as it is seen as a way of unnecessarily kowtowing to authority and trying to impress/please him/her.

Body

The content of an email needs to be concise, precise and well organised, to facilitate processing it. Though some believe in drafting extremely detailed emails, this can prove to be counterproductive, in processing and retaining the information therein.

First paragraph: What is the purpose of the email?

The initial paragraph should highlight why the email is being sent; as, being the introductory paragraph, it focuses the attention of an individual, especially if the email is long or if the receiver is very busy, thus being prone to skimming over the rest of the email.

More importantly, at the very outset, the presence of any attachment should be made evident, primarily because, while at times the presence of an attachment may skip the person's notice, at others, due to technical issues, the document may not get attached and the recipient would not realise that anything is amiss.

Second (and, if need be subsequent) paragraph(s): Details about the purpose

This would include both a detailed description/explanation of what is stated in the introductory paragraph and, if needed, information about the day and date, place and time of the event. This information (i.e. the day and date, place and time) could be listed one below the other to make it stand out and facilitate remembering it.

Third/Final paragraph: Complimentary close; statement of action expected

The third and final paragraph could include what the sender expects by way of action, in the context of the email, like,

'Could you kindly peruse the proposal and revert?'; 'Looking forward to hearing from you' etc. This could be followed by a complimentary close for example, 'Many thanks'; 'Thanking you' etc. However, this needs to be clearly followed by a sign off line and the signature.

In case there is no specific action that one expects from the receiver of the email, one can close the email merely with a complimentary close.

Sign off

The usual sign off in an email is 'Regards' though American companies often use 'Thanks and Regards'; however, while thanks is the more informal way of saying thank you, regards has a slightly higher degree of formality in word use. So too, while it is fine saying Warm regards/Kind regards, Best regards is improper as Regards are in themselves good wishes, thus making the construction awkward.

More so, though people sign off as Yours faithfully/Yours sincerely/Yours truly, these are not appropriate for the email as a form; the first two are used as formal letters sign offs, while the third is used as a sign off for informal letters.

Signature line

The signature line should contain the sender's

- name and surname as the first line

- designation and department as the second line
- organisation's name as the third line
- organisational logo and tagline – optional, as per company policies

One can also use a digital signature, between the sign off line and the first line. However, this is not necessary, as creating a digital signature poses its own challenges and has its own risks. So too, even without the digital signature all emails, except those that serve as legal documents – MOUs etc., have a legal binding.

One could also add one's contact details, i.e. office address and telephone numbers (office and cell), at the end of the signature line. But, this is not necessary; it can increase the email size and can result in unwanted details being available to others. On the other hand, though, it can serve as an easy access for a person, who may wish to access you, as s/he may not have to store your number or access your visiting card for the details.

Moreover, one can always save a signature line for one's professional email id, as this helps in preventing repetitive work of typing it in, with every email. On the flip side though, if it is saved, one has to be careful, if one is sending an informal mail to a friend/acquaintance and has the same id that one uses for personal and professional reasons, as that may result in making the receiver, who is a friend/family member feel alienated.

Often, companies follow the policy of marketing their presence and reinforcing the brand, by adding the company logo and company tagline at the end of the official mails sent by all employees. This could include lines like 'This too shall pass' (Symantec), 'Believe in the Best' (BPL) etc. However, their use in emails, even though official, is as per company policies and not at the discretion of the employees. Therefore, if it has to appear at the end of one's email, the company makes it known to the employee. Using the logo and tagline, without the company's instructions/permission, may on the other hand amount to violation of the protocol and may therefore attract action.

It is important to remember that one can vary the signature, from a long signature to a short one and an intervening one, depending on the person one is addressing and the frequency with which one writes to him/her. For example, one need not include the organisation's address, if one is writing to another person from the same organisation. So too, if it is a mail chain, one need not even include one's designation and the organisation's name, beyond the first email in the chain. However, it is not incorrect, if one sticks to a single signature; especially if it is the intervening one – i.e. the name, designation and organisation's address - of the individual.

If the content of the email is in the correct format and is properly organised, it creates a favourable impression and also makes it easier for the receiver(s), to process the information. In fact, it makes precious little sense if one has to call another person (the sender) to ask him/her to explain the meaning of the content of the email that one has sent. Care and caution should therefore be exercised in effectively using the email format, both in the context of its form and content.

Note: A detailed break-up of the matter that goes into every paragraph appears in the chapter -Types of Emails and a specimen of every type appears in the chapter - Email Specimens.

Email Features

Varied features are made available by different service providers, to make the email appear more personalised/effective. Though these need not necessarily be used, they can enhance the appearance of your email.

Since Gmail is one of the most user friendly service provider and also has many features, most of the features covered here are those that are offered by Gmail.

1. Gmail features

A. On Logging into the Account

The varied features that are listed below this head appear, when one logs into one's account. These are thus the primary/basic features of the account, most of which have to be regularly used by any email account holder.

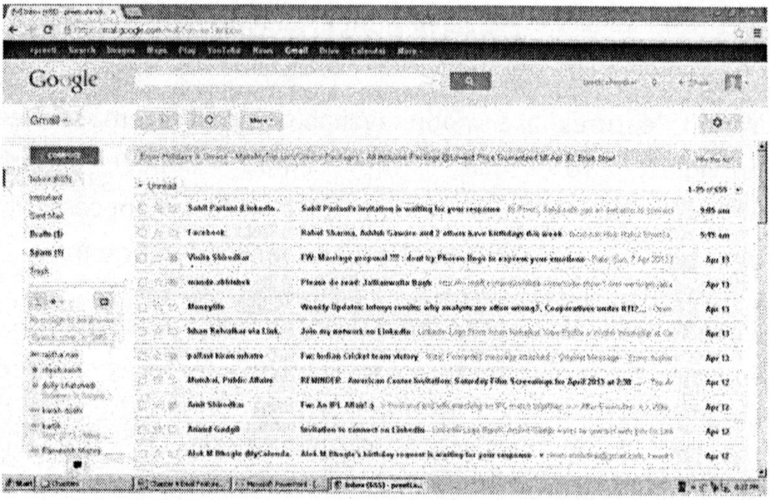

a. **Contacts:** The email account can be used to save/create one's professional and personal contact list, which could include the name, designation, address, email id and contact numbers (both landline and cell). This serves the dual purpose of having all the data recorded conveniently and in one place, so that one need not have to write it down or carry it, while yet remaining easily accessible, as one can now access email, even through tablets or mobile phones. Moreover, this data can be easily edited and has lesser chances of getting lost or destroyed, unlike when it is in the digital or in the written form.

b. **Tasks:** Explained in detail later in this chapter, tasks help one to set up 'to do' lists for oneself/others, in an organised an efficient manner, without much effort.

Moreover, a reminder of this can be sent to the receiver /oneself, by way of an email, so that the other person, as well as one, does not forget/miss out on the task.

c. **Compose:** By clicking on this button, one can draft/create an email. One would then need to fill varied details like To:, Cc:, Bcc:, Subject: and the actual mail content. In 'Compose' too, one has many other facilities that have been explained later in the chapter.

d. **Inbox:** Inbox is a folder, where all the emails, that one has received, appear. Its appearance/display can also be customised, as per one's liking; whether it is the choice of the themes, colour, number of emails per page or appearance (i.e. whether they should be displayed as per their being received or unread followed by read).

e. **Important:** Those emails that are significant, either in the context of their content or expected action can be marked as important, either by default (by the service provider) or by choice (by the receiver of the email).

f. **Sent Mail:** This folder contains all the emails that have been sent by the account holder. This can both prove to be a valuable record and a point of reference. Moreover, if the message does not get sent or if one needs to send the same message to other(s), it is useful to find it saved in the 'Sent' items.

g. **Drafts:** Those emails which need to be sent repeatedly or emails that don't get sent, either because of connectivity failure or since the sender may get busy with something else, can be saved as 'Drafts'. This helps prevent the loss of effort. Some service providers automatically save every email as a draft, till such a time it gets sent. More so, one can 'Save as Drafts' some email content that one has to regularly send, by way of personal/professional courtesies or office routine.

h. **Spam:** All emails that can either harm the computer or have content that is merely promotional or does not directly concern the receiver appear in or can be sent to the 'Spam' folder. One can choose to mark an email from the 'Spam' folder as 'Not Spam' or delete it forever. If neither of this action is performed, some service providers have the option of automatically emptying the 'Spam' folder, after a specific duration.

i. **Trash:** All the messages deleted by the account holder remain in the trash box, for a specific period of time. Furthermore, while in some cases, one has to empty the trash folder oneself, in others the trash gets automatically deleted, after a specific period of time. It is sometimes helpful that an email one has deleted from the inbox remains in/goes to the 'Trash' folder, as it may have been deleted by mistake or one may need to access it, in certain unforeseeable situations or for reference.

j. **Circles:** This provides one the facility of creating groups of one's email contacts. These groups can appear under the heads

- **Personal:** For family and friends
- **Travel:** For those one travels with for professional reasons
- **More:** Any other group that one may wish to form. One can also give such a group an Indicative title.

k. **Chat:** The chat window gives the account holder the option for instant messaging, where a separate window pops up and one can, in real time, engage in a written conversation/idea exchange with another. One can also simultaneously chat with varied people on different chat windows. This helps, especially if one is working together, on some project, and needs real-time idea exchange or wishes to network.

l. **Hangout:** An email version of tele/video conferencing, though the word hangout may sound informal, this option provides the facility of interacting simultaneously with numerous people for professional/personal reasons.

m. **Select:** By clicking on select, one can mark with a tick all emails (all), remove the ticks one has inserted (none), or mark them as read, unread, starred, unstarred. This in turn would help one act further upon these emails (marked by a tick). For example, one could select all starred emails and archive them or delete them, if one has completed the tasks that one has decided. This option thus helps in saving time, by clubbing all emails of a type together, for common action, thereby forestalling having to perform a chosen action, on one email at a time.

n. **Refresh:** If one's account is idle or if one learns that a new email has been sent, but is not reflecting in the inbox, one can click on 'refresh'. This helps in reloading the email account, bringing it up-to-date till that actual moment.

o. **More**

These connote the additional features that are available, though they may not be frequently used.

i. **Mark all as Read:** This makes all the emails appear as 'read'. Usually one would not use this option, as one deliberately leaves the unread emails highlighted (marked as unread), as they thereby automatically get highlighted and draw one's attention. However, if one has received only a few emails, on a particular day, and they are ones that one has read before or emails the content of which one is familiar with, one could mark them as unread. Before using this option however one only needs to ensure that there are no former pending emails that are marked as unread.

p. Settings

This covers the options available to the person with an email account, in the context of the appearance of his/her account.

- **Display density**: This helps one to choose how many emails one needs to appear at a glance, when one opens one's inbox. The options available are 'comfortable', 'cozy', 'compact' – the former showing the display with about 50 emails appearing on a page, on scroll, while in 'compact' they appear in a smaller size, with 'cozy' offering an in-between size, so that a person can choose the look, based on one's level of comfort with the size of the font, in which they are displayed.
- **Settings:** A system setting option, this gives the user a wide range of options that helps him/her choose and customise the operations of the account as per one's need. For example, one can change the language to UK English, rather than the default US English, especially if one prefers British English over American English. So too, one can activate 'recall mail' from here, so that one can retrieve and cancel an email one has sent to another, if the receiver hasn't accessed it till then/within a certain time limit.
- **Themes:** One can choose the appearance of the email display through themes. These offer a range of colours and designs, making it attractive for the younger generation, for whom the email account is a personal statement and not merely an aid facilitating correspondence.

- **Feedback:** This provides the user with the option of providing feedback to Google, about their products, so that they can offer the best services to their clients. This is especially useful, since Google offers a range of products from blog-sites, documents to search engines, email, maps, translator and others.
- **Help:** Any query that one may have about a product or feature can be resolved, by accessing help and reading the information provided therein or then typing a question and searching for the answer to it. This facilitates a novice, in making the most of the features available and the constant additions made to them.

q. **View Profile:** By selecting 'View Profile', one can edit one's personal details and/or upload a photograph, so that these get reflected the other features like 'chat', 'circles' etc.

r. **Search:** One can use the option of 'Search' to find old emails from one's account (inbox, sent, drafts, trash and spam). This could include a search based on sender, receiver, subject or any word in the content. On clicking on this option, all the emails and their locations (inbox, sent, drafts, trash and spam) appear as a list, which makes it easy for one to locate the email.

B. *In 'Compose'*

The varied features that are listed below this head appear, when one clicks on 'Compose', in order to draft an email to send someone. These features are therefore related to and useful in creating/drafting emails.

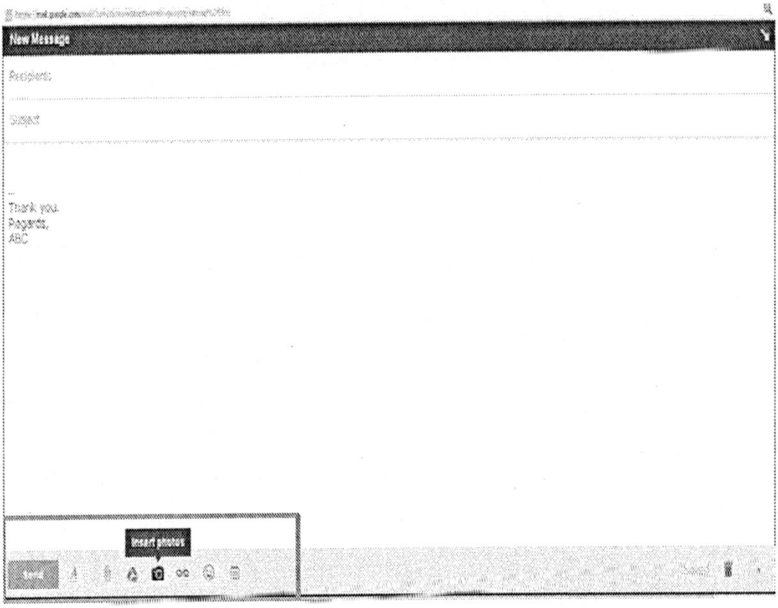

a. Formatting options

Using these one can format the email content to make it appear better/more organised. These appear as a band at the bottom of the email and are hidden on the band, to avoid clutter, while yet being easily accessible.

i. **Font**: The type of font used should suit the content, yet be easily 'readable'. Thus, most emails/documents use Times New Roman and Calibri for official content, as they are easy on the eyes. Moreover, one should use fonts that are commonly available, as the message may otherwise appear garbled.

ii. **Size**: The size should neither be too small, to avoid making reading it difficult, or too large, making it appear 'too much in the face'/unnecessarily prominent and therefore 'loud'. Size 12 in most common official fonts is considered appropriate. However, size suitability would vary as per the nature of the font.

iii. **Bold**: Needs to be used only if there are various headings/sub headings in one's emails. What one needs to remember is that too much bold can result only in putting off the reader and so must be used extremely sparingly.

iv. **Italics**: Matter in italics helps to draw attention to the text, while at the same time being subdued, rather than flashy. Moreover, it is a writing convention to put titles of books and texts in italics, in running matter, so as to make them stand apart from the rest of the text.

v. **Underline**: Underlining a point is also a subtle way of drawing attention to a part of the content. However, care should be taken that not more than a couple of words or a sentence or two are underlined, as otherwise the matter can look extremely cluttered to the eye; so too, underlining far too much would make the very fact of underlining lose its significance.

vi. **Text colour**: The text colour can be changed, to highlight content. However, the colour needs to be sober and suited to the content.

vii. **Numbered list/Bulleted list**: Numbers/bullets are used to organise matter under varied sub-heads, especially if they are different but related points. While a numbered list helps, when the points move as steps or in a serial order; a bulleted list is useful in all other contexts. More so, a bulleted list appears more mature/formal than a numbered list, which may have a fairly childish appearance.

viii. **Align**: Content that is shabby in appearance can put off the reader, thereby undervaluing the importance of the content. Aligning content, at a very basic level, creates an impression of neatness. Moreover, if one is using large amount of text as quotes, it is an accepted practice to indent the matter. Indenting sub-points also helps in making them stand out, thereby drawing one's attention to them.

ix. **Remove formatting**: After having formatted the text, if one is not pleased with the visual effect that the formatting has created, one can remove the entire formatting on the click of this button.

b. **Attach files**: All files that need to be sent as attachments can be added on, by selecting them one after the other, after clicking on the attach button. However, care needs to be taken that the files are in fact attached, as the process may not get completed, especially if the connection is slow or one loses the network, even if for a brief moment; that the names given to the file are indicative of the content in it, rather than being ambiguous or generic; that the attached files are saved in a lower/compatible version, so that the receiver has no issues accessing them; that they are in an easy access format and do not require an unusual software or specialised knowledge for access; and, that the route is not unnecessarily long, so that the file name gets unnecessary additions in its title route.

For example, if one is editing a file that someone has already sent, it is better to add the word edited before re-sending it, so as to forestall confusion – 'Republic Day Speech' can be renamed 'Edited Republic Day Speech', or rather than calling your bio data merely 'Resume', it is better to use the title 'Resume Prayag Chaturvedi'

c. **Insert files using drive:** One can insert any number of files from one's computer, without having to go through the process of attaching them, one at a time. By clicking on this link, one can merely drag and drop all the files that one wishes to send and then click on the upload button. All the files then appear in the text box of 'compose' and can be sent (unlike attachments, which reflect separately and may therefore be missed by the recipient) to as many recipients as one may desire. This can prove especially fast and useful ,if one has to send a lot of files, as also when one wants to ensure that the receiver does not miss out on them.

d. **Insert photos:** One can directly insert a photo in the compose box, by clicking on this icon. This can save the trouble of going through numerous steps, to upload photos.

e. **Insert links:** One can add a link providing the website details, to which the url should go and the text that one may want to represent it by; so that one can directly insert the link and send it to the person one wishes to. In turn, the recipient can directly access that url/website, by merely clicking on the link, rather than having to cut-paste/type it in a separate window.

f. **Insert smiley:** One can insert emoticons/smileys (face outlines that reflect varied emotions), to represent the emotions that one may want to convey, but may not be able to effectively capture in words. However, one should not insert smileys in formal emails.

g. **Insert invitation:** One can insert an invitation to various events, specifying basic details like when, where, what. This will not only create a reminder in the sender as well as receiver's calendar, but will also create an email reminder. Moreover, sending an invite in this manner also provides scope to directly get a response (RSVP), about whether the person would be joining the event and whether s/he would be getting anyone else along, thus making keeping tabs on the information convenient, for both the sender and the receiver.

h. **Discard draft:** If one needs to discard the whole email that one has composed, for any reason whatsoever, one can directly press on 'Discard draft', which will delete it totally, thus preventing wastage of time, in deleting it part by part.

i. **Temporarily switch back to old compose:** The above mentioned features in 'Compose', being a part of the new look being offered, can at times create disorientation, since one may not have become accustomed to them. To deal with just such an issue, there is an option of switching back to the old compose, which may offer lesser features, but a greater sense of comfort, since one is more used to it.

j. **Label**: Explained in detail later, under the head 'labels/move to', this option provides the scope of putting the composed mail into various folders, making categorisation and access simpler.

k. **Print**: One can directly print an email, by pressing on the print button, without having to go through numerous steps that would be otherwise involved in printing the document.

l. **Check Spelling**: This option allows one to run a spell check on the document, which can help both in the case that one is not very proficient with spellings or in case one is in a hurry or is tired, which may both result in missing out on spelling errors.

C. On opening an email from the 'Inbox'

The varied features that are listed below this head appear, when one clicks on 'Inbox', and opens the email(s), one has received. These features are therefore related to and useful in accessing/storing emails.

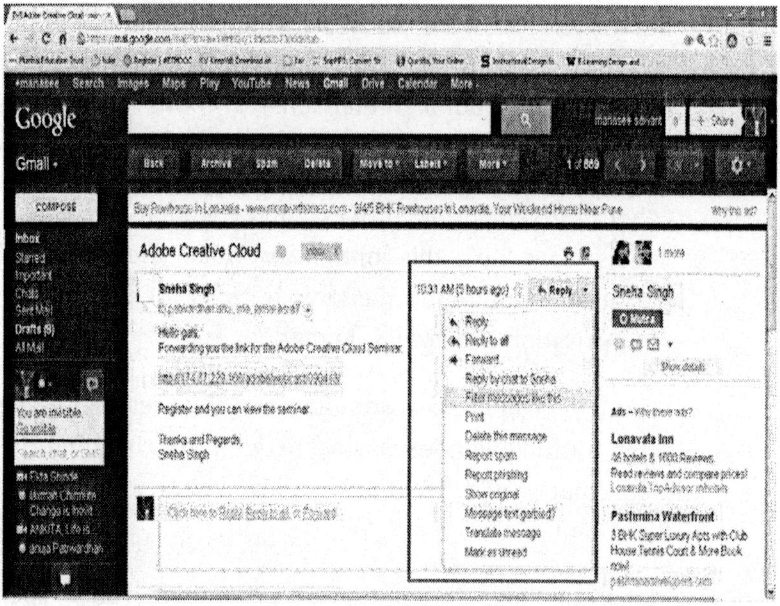

a. **Back to Inbox**: Usually after opening an email, if one returns to the inbox, depending upon the display option, one has chosen, the email goes to the top of the 'read' section, while the 'unread' section remains on the top. However, if one were to click on the 'Back to Inbox' button, it takes one back directly to the inbox, with the emails appearing in the order in which they have been delivered to the inbox.

b. **Archive:** This button enables one to archive (store) the email for future reference. Thus de-cluttering the inbox.

c. **Report Spam:** By clicking on this button, after one has opened the email, one can directly send the email to spam, where all the emails that are suspect appear, either since one has marked them as spam or by automatic filtering that is offered by the service provider.

d. **Delete:** One can delete the email(s) one does not want to store, by clicking on this button, to prevent clutter in the inbox and avoid unnecessary use of email space. This is because not all service providers make unlimited space available; and so, if there is unnecessary storing, one may lose out on important emails. So too, searching for a specific email from the clutter may prove highly difficult and time consuming.

e. **Labels/Move to**

While 'labels' means that one can create folders with the mentioned labels and can transfer all related email into them, the 'move to' option helps one moving the marked/identified emails to that particular folder. These are emails that one would want to store, without them generally cluttering the inbox. So too, labelling them/putting them in folders would make them easier to find, if one needs to access them again and they have been sent by a person, with whom one exchanges emails at a highly regular frequency.

The labels/folders available are

- **Personal** : Those related to an individual's life or are those concerning one's family or friends.
- **Receipts**: These would include numerous e-docs, i.e. documents that are sent by various companies in the form of soft copies/scanned copies (e.g. bank statements, insurance receipts etc.).
- **Travel**: Documents /itinerary that are related to one's travel plans, which may include e-tickets, schedules etc.
- **Work**: Information related to work that one may need to store for a variety of reasons, including legal implications/value.
- **Spam**: Emails whose content is suspect and can harm one's life/computer.
- **Trash:** Emails that need to be deleted from the inbox, but which one may not want to get rid of totally. If one puts them in the trash folder, they remain there for a month and are then permanently deleted, automatically.
- **Create New:** One can create labels as per one's specific requirements, so that can categorise emails according to one's need.
- **Manage Labels:** This provides one with the option of showing, hiding and dealing with emails, from a system point of view.

f. More

Under this head, one can find features that are fairly useful, though not always used, since they are not needed for basic email use.

- **Mark as unread:** If one wants to return to an email one has read, in order to act upon it, at a later point, one can mark it as unread, by clicking upon this button, so that one notices it among the unread emails, every time one accesses the inbox.
- **Mark as important:** At times, the service providers mark certain emails as important, by putting an arrow beside them, by automatically filtering them and deciding their importance, based upon the sender (the frequency with which s/he send one emails) or words/subject (as per the value that they/it suggest(s); i.e. an email with 'Resume' in its subject will get marked as important, while 'Funny' will not). However, one can also choose to mark an email as important, based on the value one accords to it.
- **Add to tasks:** If one needs to schedule action for some of the emails, one has received; especially those related to office work, one can add them to tasks, by clicking on this button. Moreover, one can add a subject, date, notes etc. and email this to the concerned people, including oneself, so that one is reminded of the pending tasks, when one logs in and activates the inbox.
- **Add star:** One can mark an email with add star (in which case a star will appear beside it in the display of the inbox), if one desires to accord it a special status. These may be emails reflecting occasions, events etc., that are highly important in one's professional/personal space. While 'mark as important' is usually an automatic service, as a result of which, emails appear in the inbox marked as important; 'add star' is usually an option that is exercised

by the receiver of the email and is used most often after the email is read.

- **Create event:** In order to schedule a meeting/function etc., one can use the option 'create event', which can send and record the event, along with the time., date etc., and send out an email in this regard, helping one save a lot of time and procedure.
- **Filter messages like these:** If one wants to search for messages of a certain kind/belonging to the same area/ containing similar subject matter, one can do so by choosing the 'filter messages like these' option. This would help one see all the emails of a particular nature together. For example, if one wishes to find all emails related to a project, one is working on, which may been sent to/received from people, one can choose this option.
- **Mute:** Those emails that need to remain in the inbox, but should not appear there, in case the email is hacked or accessed by another person, since the matter in the email is confidential, can be marked as 'mute'. This helps them to remain hidden, so that nobody, other than the person who has marked them as 'mute', is aware of their presence. If one needs to search for these emails, one can type the sender's name or date on which the email has been received or subject in the search option, at the top of the email box, and the email becomes visible. One also has a choice of removing the 'mute' option, so that the email is automatically reflected again, in the inbox.

g. **Attachments:** Attachments, in the form of documents/photos, serve to send/access matter that has already been created, in some other format. On receiving an attachment, one can either choose to view it or download it.

- **View:** This opens the document/photograph in another window and should be used, if one merely wishes to see/peruse it.
- **Download:** This downloads/copies the document/photograph on one's computer/ hand-held device and should be used if one wishes to save/reuse it.

h. **Reply:** Instead of going again into 'compose' or clicking on the 'reply' or 'reply all' that appears at the bottom of an email, one can use this option to reply to the sender of the email.

i. **Forward:** One can use this button to forward an email (send the same email) to another person(s), by merely adding the recipient and any content one wishes to. This helps in reducing the steps that one may take in sending forwards.

j. **Report phishing:** If an email has a request to divulge some personal information, one can mark it as a phishing attack. In this case, the entire text message goes to the google (back end) team, who can take action to prevent further such attacks. This may include the sender's emails being blocked or getting marked as spam.

k. **Show original:** The html version (backend version – as it appears before being coded for sending) gets reflected, on clicking on this button. Though this is not much relevant to an average email user, it can prove to be useful for people from the field of information technology or computer applications or in case the email gets reported, as a cyber crime.

l. **Message text garbled?:** If the text of the email cannot be read, due to font incompatibility, using this option can enable one to see the message in a font that is compatible with one's computer. However, all the formatting disappears and the images, if any, do not appear in this version.

m. **Translate message:** By selecting this option, one can translate the basic text of the email into another language. This option lists a lot of international languages that serve as a national language (the official language of a nation), from which one can choose. One can use this to decode a message, if it appears in a language, one does not understand.

2. Other advanced features

Certain features of the email can help enhance productivity, mainly in the context of those who use email excessively, especially in the professional sphere. However, these features are not always used, though they are gaining popularity, among the younger generation. From among the many that fall into this category, a couple are briefly mentioned below, as the others as well as the details of these two would become rather technical.

- **Sync with other accounts**: Gmail offers the facility of synchronising all other email accounts of an individual, with his/her Gmail account. If one makes use of this facility, one can get all the emails that one receives, in any one of one's numerous accounts, in the inbox of the Gmail account. This helps in creating a one-point access, for the account holder, so that one does not need to unnecessarily occupy one's time, in opening numerous email accounts. However, this defeats the very purpose of having numerous accounts and can also cause a clutter, making it difficult to separate the personal from professional emails, thus creating the possibility of missing out on some important piece of communication.

- **Mail merge**: When one is accessing the email, one is in fact, using up internet time, in order to access one's email account, which is located on a 'cloud'. This can not only increase the cost, spent on internet access, but also result in speed fluctuation for access, as internet speed may vary, at different times and locations. To avoid this from happening, one can use, the Pop and Imap services offered by Outlook, Lotus and Thunderbird, for computer use. Based on this, one can sync one's account and one would keep getting the updated version of one's email account directly on one's computer, without having to log in. One can then perform the desired actions, and the account will automatically sync it with the active email account. Since this is done offline i.e. off the internet, it proves both faster and more cost efficient. The same facility is even available on IOS or Android enabled hand-held devices.

3. Features that are not in Gmail

Receipt on delivery and Receipt on reading: A feature not available in Gmail, this is nevertheless extremely useful, as one can have a receipt sent to one's email account, on delivery or read of the email, so that one knows that one's email has reached the person, without him/her necessarily sending a response. While the receipt on delivery gets generated automatically, the receiver is left with the option of choosing, whether s/he wants the receipt to be sent to the sender.

Though not a part of basic email sending, a knowledge of and use of these features can simplify life, make email drafting simpler, customise the emails as per one's requirement and increase overall proficiency. In this light, features remain an evolving, enchanting and enticing part of the email world.

Email functions

The basic purpose of an email is to serve as a convenient and speedy means of written communication and it thus often used as a modern replacement of the letter/mail, as the very name suggests. However, over a span of time, as it has evolved and begun offering greater facilities, due to the ingenuity of the service providers, whose chief aim it is to attract the largest account holder base, the email has acquired varied functions. The features offered are thus numerous, diverse and ever increasing; and if used effectively, they can help one, not only in gaining maximum benefit and effectiveness, but also in addressing numerous issues, whether of easy access or security.

File storage

Most office routine/tasks require a lot of paper work that needs to be stored as record, in case any legal complications arise. The email offers an easy solution to this, as email correspondence has a legal standing; so also, papers can be scanned and stored on the email, thus preventing their getting lost or frayed with time. Moreover, unlike on the computer or on storage devices (like the pen drive, compact disc – cd or external hard disk), data stored on the email has no fear of getting lost due to technical failure (like the hard disk crashing or the pen drive getting corrupted). The only chance of data loss could be through account hacking, the chances of which could be minimised, by following internet security protocol.

Archiving

Emails or important documents, whether personal or professional, can be archived in the email and accessed as per one's convenience. They can also be deleted or edited as and when their utility is over. The email thus basically serves as an easy access portfolio of all of one's important documents, so that they can be stored safely and accessed from anywhere. So too, all important emails that contain content that may have legal implications or would be required at a later point in time can be archived, retrieved and easily accessed from one's email account. The archiving facility thus offers an easy and safe option, for matter that one considers important.

Document sharing

While working in teams, colleagues often need to share data/documents that they work on simultaneously. At such times, working on hard copies can lead to not only wasting a lot of paper but also result in creating confusion, by creating multiple copies of the same document and the resultant possibility of missing out incorporating some important information into the final document. At such times, certain service providers afford the facility of sharing the document via the email, where the person, who creates the document, can choose whether to merely share the document with the others or offer them the scope to edit it, thereby making the process of working simultaneously on a document much simpler. Moreover, the alerts about such documents are reflected in the inbox, facilitating the team effort even further.

Contact back up

The email account is a fairly safe (if one follows the security protocol of the web) and reliable space for storing contact details of colleagues/family members and friends, including not merely their email id (which can be automatically stored, depending upon the service provider), but also their addresses and telephone numbers, so that one gets rid of traditional storage devices like diaries or digital diaries that can get worn out, lost or may become non-functional. Moreover, being in the virtual space the contact data base on the email is not merely easily accessible, but constitutes a more or less a permanent record that can be edited, without too much effort, making it a complete record that remains with you, unless one is caught in the eventuality of one's account being hacked/frozen, the latter being a remote possibility, considering the unlimited space that most service providers make available.

Invitations

The email can be used to send customised invitations for personal/professional functions, to numerous people, at the same time, at a convenient and fast pace. Moreover, those who receive the invitation can choose to reply, about their presence/absence, as well as whether they would be coming alone or would be accompanied by others, by simply clicking on the options provided in the invite, which get collated and delivered to the original sender as an email. This confirmation, in turn, can help the sender of the invitation to plan the event and manage it logistically. So too, the date can be marked in the calendar of the sender as well as receiver, so that they would not miss out on the event; especially, given that most individuals now have their email accounts in sync with their hand held devices – whether tablets or mobile phones.

Reminders

Reminders about various events or special dates like the birthdays/anniversaries of family members/friends/colleagues are easily available on one's email, where the reminder pops up and one has the choice of even sending e-greetings. This in turn takes the stress out of remembering things or the need of having to carry a planner and makes networking as well as not missing out on important personal/professional commitments that much easier.

Being aware of the varied functions of the email can result in optimum utilisation of this mode of communication, making it serve the sender as well as the receiver in numerous ways.

TOTAL:

Amount in Words:
Two Hundred Seventy only

Whether tax is payable under reverse charge - No

*ASSPL-Amazon Seller Services Pvt. Ltd., ARIPL-Amazon Retail India Pvt. L

Please note that this invoice

Email Safeguards

Often remembering and working upon certain highly basic security measures can make email use fairly safe and can prevent hacking/data loss, which is one of the primary reasons that people are wary about saving extremely important personal/professional data/documents online.

Keeping the password complicated

It is believed that a password should be long and a blend of letters of the alphabet and numbers, so that it becomes difficult to hack, through experimentation. And while one feels that the password should include one's name, the name of one's loved ones, date of birth/age of the self/loved ones, in order to make it easy to remember; this should be avoided at all costs, since that makes the password easy for others to guess/hack.

Not replicating the password

Often for the sake of convenience in remembering, one uses the same password for varied/multiple email accounts or numerous operations requiring the internet, including ebanking. While this no doubt sounds convenient, it also makes hacking into accounts easy; as, if one account is hacked, hacking all the others will become that much simpler. So also, in inevitable/exceptional circumstances, if one has to reveal the password to a colleague/family member/friend, s/he would have access to all of one's accounts.

Not disclosing the password

One should not let one's password be known to family, friends or colleagues either so that one can ask them for it, in case one forgets or in order to access one's account, in an 'urgent' situation. Moreover, if this just has to be done on an exceptional occasion, one needs to immediately/at the first opportune moment change one's password.

Changing the password frequently

Keeping the same password, over a long period of time, makes it more prone to getting hacked. Therefore, it is sensible to change one's password, at least once in three months, if not every month.

Keeping a separate email id for the team

It can often happen that something urgent can crop up, when one is not in office and/or does not have access to the email. At such times, one's boss may expect the work, which is urgent, to be carried forward by one's colleagues/team members. In such circumstances, one may be forced to reveal one's password to other members of the team; and, while one can change the password soon thereafter, one is still exposed to the risk of the colleagues accessing the account repeatedly, till the password is changed or going through other emails in one's inbox, that one may not want them to access. It is therefore important to have a team id, so that the sender can be asked to copy the mail to the team id.

Do not keep the account open/idling for long

People often log into their account in the morning and stay logged on throughout the day/for long periods, during which they are not actually accessing the email. This makes it easy for professional hackers to hack into one's account and then change the password, thereby taking the account over. It is therefore important to log in and log out as many times as one may need to; keeping the account in an 'open' state, only as long as one is accessing the id.

Ensure that the be/stay signed in box is not checked

Most email service providers have the option of 'be/stay signed in' on the email account. This is to facilitate prevention of repeated terminating of sessions, if the account is open but in an idle state. While some service providers make this a 'check the box' activity, where one needs to check the box, if one wants to remain signed in, other service providers make it a default tick i.e. one remains signed in automatically, unless one chooses to unclick the box. One needs to be careful to observe, which of these options has been provided by one's service provider; and in case of the latter, one needs to, on every occasion, check that the box offering the 'be/stay signed in' option is unclicked. If one fails to do this, then one would remain logged into one's account, without realising it. This is especially risky, in case one shares one's computer/laptop with another.

Do not accept the 'remember password' request

Service providers, at times, give the option of 'remember password - now or never'. It is necessary to tick on the 'never' option in such cases, because, one would otherwise get automatically logged in from that particular computer/laptop immediately on feeding in the email id, which too appears as an option in a drop down box, if one feeds the first letter of the email id, in case if one is using the desktop/laptop frequently, a facility made available for the convenience of the user, since the email ids are often long, so one need not have to type them every time.

Do not save/record passwords in an accessible place

Phones, desktops or even inboxes are not places, where one should store one's email id, along with the password or by itself. This is because, if the phone is lost or stolen or the account is hacked, this information becomes easy to access. If at all, such information needs to be stored in a password enabled document, which would make it difficult to access this sensitive information.

Ensure that the other person is not attempting to view your password

While one is logging into one's account, in the presence of other(s), whether on a personal desktop or laptop or, more especially so, in a cyber café, one should be careful that one is not being closely watched. This is because people, who are adept in computer usage malpractices, can easily figure out the password, by looking at one's finger movement over the keys.

Ensure that the password in not getting typed in the id box

Especially when one is in a hurry or is multitasking, one may forget to move from the id box to the password box, after one has keyed in/selected one's email id. This would mean that the password gets typed in the id box and is therefore revealed, as it will get reflected in its actual form (the letters/word gets typed out as it is), rather than as a code, as it does in the password box.

Make the password retrieval system foolproof

One is given the option of basing password retrieval on a question, the answer of which would remind one of one's password. The other option that is given is that of providing another account id of oneself, to which the password would be sent in case one clicks on the 'forgot password' option. If one is using the 'forgot password' option, one should ensure that the question is such that it should remind one of the correct answer, especially if it is chosen from a pre-given set of options, rather than being a question that one can word as per one's requirement. So too, in case of the latter, one should be careful that the id one provides is one that is active and personal. This is because if one fails to do so and one cannot retrieve the password of one's account, which one has forgotten, it would mean that the account becomes inaccessible permanently; and if one had saved confidential data in it, that data would be lost forever.

Masking the confidential information stored / archived / muted in the email

There is no doubt that the email can be a safe and secure place for storing information, since it is online and the information is not capable of getting destroyed/lost, in any way, other than by hacking. However, if one's account is hacked, this confidential information could become easily accessible to the hacker and therefore liable to be misused. Hence, one needs to save this confidential information, whether it is stored in the inbox, archived or muted, either in the form of a code (e.g. rather than saving *icici debit card password - 8876* one could save it as *idbp8876*) or by way of an attachment that is password enabled and therefore unlikely to be accessed, even if the account is hacked.

Additionally, it is better to save such a mail as muted, rather than archived or stored since at first glance, no one would be in a position to see the presence of a muted mail, making misusing it harder.

Do not share the password on other sites

Many sites (including professional websites like LinkedIn)/spam emails ask passwords of other accounts/email accounts. One really needs to check/be aware of the veracity of such claims, before one reveals one's passwords. Thus, while linking one's email account on another professional website would be relatively safe, it would be totally unsafe to reveal one's passwords on a spam mail. So too, if one has linked one's email account to another account, it would be better not to save any confidential data in such an email account, just in order to be really safe.

It is most often better to err on the cautious side, rather than risk losing one's confidential information, or having to go through the inconvenience of having one's account hacked, as one may have given the contact id to numerous people and one would therefore not only lose a lot of data and contacts, but one would also not be able to get the same id again, adding to one's woes. Hence, it is simpler to follow the safeguards that would enable greater security for one's email account.

Types of Email

The content of the email is entirely determined by why one is sending the email, the relationship one shares with the recipient and whether it is an email that one has drafted, is replying to or one that is merely being forwarded. And, while the choice of vocabulary would keep changing, even in these contexts, depending upon who the intended recipient is, it is easy to draft an effective email efficiently, if one is aware of the type of email one is drafting.

Orientation of the email

- **Original**

  If the email is original i.e. is originating from the self or is a reply (as against being a forward), the subject line and content would be shaped accordingly. It would be more detailed and would orient the person to the context of the email, if any (for example, apropos our discussion).

- **Forward**

  If the email is a forward, the subject needs to be edited, as the word 'Fwd:' will otherwise keep appearing at the beginning of the subject line, as many times as the email gets forwarded. Moreover, this creates a very poor impression and can make it appear as if the content is nothing important – it is merely forwarded and therefore not of much consequence, resulting in it being ignored/not given priority/being kept for reading in the spare time by the receiver.

So also, it is important to add a line about why one is forwarding the email, at the beginning of the email, if one is forwarding the email as itself, i.e. just as it is sent to one, merely by pressing the forward button. This could be just a line or could follow the specified content format, depending upon the relationship one shares with the person, who is to receive the email. If the relationship with the receiver of the email is very formal, it is better to follow the total email format, whereas for formal or semiformal relationships, even in a professional set up, one can include a line at the beginning of the email.

So too, one might forward the email as an attachment. In this case, the regular email format needs to be followed.

Unnecessary forwards, especially of jokes and other general information should be avoided, in a professional setting, unless it has specific value for the intended recipient. For example, if it is a cartoon that a person can use for his/her PPTs or if it is a forward on ways to treat arthritis and one's colleague, with whom one shares a good rapport has been complaining about suffering from it, one can send the forward; otherwise the former would be considered a waste of time, while the latter would be looked upon as improper professional behaviour/meddling in the personal affairs of a colleague.

Relationship with the sender

- **Formal/Semi formal**

  The salutation, the content as well as the sign off will entirely depend upon the relationship one shares with the intended recipient of the email. It is important to remember that general content or forwards should never be sent in an official context, to those with whom one shares a strictly formal relationship.

  While formal relationships denote all relationships with one's seniors, semi formal relationships can be with those working at the same level as oneself or those working as subordinates. Semi formal relations imply going beyond exchanging pleasantries, to chitchatting on issues that go beyond mere office protocol. It is not infrequent to find strong semi formal relations with one's colleagues, as most of one's waking day is spent at the workplace.

Purpose

- **Requesting**

  The request one may desire to make may take different forms – inviting a person, seeking an approval, asking the person to take some action

  a. Inviting

  - Para One: Context of the invite (whether the sender has spoken to the receiver earlier; whether the person is inviting the other based on reference) and what one is inviting the other person for
  - Para Two onwards: The details about the organisation and the programme. This could also be in the form of a list appearing one below the other, for greater clarity. (For example, the day and date, the venue and time of the programme)
  - Final paragraph: Urging the person to accept ; complimentary close

  b. Approval

  - Para One: What one is seeking approval for
  - Para Two onwards: Details related to the approval

- o Final paragraph: The course of action that one desires the other person to take, if any; complimentary close

c. **Action**
   - o Para One: What the problem/issue is
   - o Para Two onwards: The details related to the problem/issue
   - o Final paragraph: Requesting the person to act; complimentary close

- **Responding**
  - o Para One: Indication that one has read the email
  - o Para Two onwards: The course of action that one intends taking on it
  - o Final paragraph: Expectation of action, if any; complimentary close

- **Informing**
  - o Para One: What one is informing the other person about
  - o Para Two onwards: The details related to the information. This could also be in the form of a list appearing one below the other, for greater clarity. (For example, if it is a meeting – the day and date, the venue and time of

the meeting; if about one's absence from work - the duration of one's absence, the reason for one's absence and who, if anyone, would be responsible for one's work, during one's absence)

- Final paragraph: The course of action that one desires the other person to take, if any; complimentary close

- **Apologising**
  - Para One: Acceptance of error and reason for apology
  - Para Two onwards: Reason for error/misbehaviour for which one is apologising
  - Final paragraph: Request for being forgiven/being excused/exempted/ pardoned; complimentary close

- **Thanking**
  - Para One: Reason for gratitude
  - Para Two onwards: One's feelings
  - Final paragraph: Complimentary close

- **Connecting**
    - Para One: On what grounds (if one has a reference; has met the person before)/why is one connecting
    - Para Two onwards: What is/are one's expectation(s)
    - Final paragraph: Expectation of action, if any/expression of gratitude; complimentary close

- **Reporting (daily message chain)**
  This type of email needs to be as brief as possible and should strictly follow a predetermined format, so as not to waste the other person's time, since it is on an extremely regular basis.

    - Para One: What one is reporting about
    - Para Two onwards: Details of what has happened/transpired (between the last email and the current email)
    - Final paragraph: Expectation of action, if any; complimentary close

- **Office protocol/initiatives**
  These are various 'connecting/feel good initiatives' that may be taken by an organisation. This may include thought for the day; season's greetings;

birthday greetings; commendations for success; motivational emails to team members, etc. However, care should be taken that one does not use this unnecessarily, as it can otherwise be a nuisance. So too, they have to be as precise as possible and should follow email etiquette.

Some offices also follow, as protocol, sending all routine correspondence as emails – requisitions, leave applications, attendance recording issues, etc.

Keeping one's focus on the type of email that one desires to send will not merely save the time and energy of both the sender and receiver, but will also enhance the worth of the communication, by reducing/eliminating barriers and helping the email achieve its goal.

Email Etiquette

Like most forms of communication, there are no specified/declared norms to follow, as a matter of protocol, in communication through emails. However, over and above being courteous, email etiquette or its absence can create a lasting impression about the sender; especially since email communication offers adequate scope to the sender, to compose an email and carefully peruse it, before it is sent. So also, an email is not accompanied by any other aspects of communication, like non-verbal cues and variations in tone, pitch and diction that can offer the receiver additional insights in decoding what is communicated. Moreover, unlike general belief, email etiquette is really simple to follow and needs a basic awareness and exercising of caution, for effective implementation. On the other hand, the results it can yield can be tremendous.

In fact, with some of the members of the younger generation, which grows up using computers, it is easy to fall into the belief that one knows everything there is to know about drafting an email. What is not realised, however, is that there is a great deal of difference in sending emails to family and friends and sending them in a professional space. While a faux pas in the former can be laughed off or can cause some basic cooling off of relations for a brief period, the latter might result in serious consequences that may, at times, be irreversible.

- **Know the recipients**

  The content of an email as well as the vocabulary used should be entirely dependent upon the receiver(s) and the relationship the sender shares with him/her/them. And while using casual language, emoticons, short forms, one liners etc. are fine in an informal email, in a formal email, they are just not acceptable. In fact, in order to modify/select the content and vocabulary of the email, based on the recipients, the cultural context, age, gender, position and how long one has known the recipient should all serve as decisive factors.

  Thus 'hey/hi' is an improper salutation in a formal email; so too, while one can use 'it was great seeing you after a long time' or 'thanks' in a semi formal relation, it would be more appropriate to use 'it was a pleasure to have met you' or 'thank you', in the case of relationships that are extremely formal.

- **Introduce yourself**

  If one is sending an email to an unknown contact that one has learnt of or to unknown recipients, it is important to introduce oneself, (name designation and area of work) as well as the organisation, if need be. One cannot expect a favourable response from the recipient(s), if one does not basically know the person, who has sent the email, or the organisation s/he represents.

- **Respond in a timely manner**

  It is important to respond in a minimum time span to the email of another, at least to inform him/her that one has received it, even though it may take a while to act upon it, due to the nature of the request made. A respectable time span, in which to respond, is usually considered to be 24 hours after receipt of the email, unless there are a couple of public holidays or weekends that follow the email. Moreover, if one is travelling/ has no access to email, one has the option of activating the automated out-of-office reply that most email service providers offer. This would ensure that there is no misunderstanding and that the person is aware that the mail has reached the desired recipient.

- **Avoid using capital letters**

  An email in all capital letters or entire sentences or words in capital letters is equated to 'shouting' in email language. Unlike what is believed, neither of this serves to draw attention to the line or the email or add value to it, in any manner. It only appears to the receiver as an act or rudeness, which is bound to result in a lot of miscommunication and misunderstanding. It is important to understand, in this context, that it is not merely the choice of words that defines the tone and politeness of the message.

- **No unnecessary forwards**

  It is not uncommon to receive/send an email, which has as its subject line FWD:FWD:FWD:FWD and the actual subject. This is because people have the habit of randomly forwarding emails they like, find interesting or amusing to everybody in their contact list.

  So too, people often feel that they are being extremely cautious, when they forward an email to others, especially in official matters, as they feel that these people should be in the know of the issue under consideration.

  However, most people have a busy working schedule and often do not get the time to go through unnecessary forwards. Moreover, they uselessly consume time in opening/deleting them and left unattended/unread, these emails can clutter the inbox, creating issues of space or resulting in reduction of visibility of what may be left/arrive in the inbox, as an important email. So too, if one desires to keep people in the loop, there one can always include them in the Cc column.

  In case, if one has to forward a message or forward a forward, for unavoidable reasons, it is necessary to edit the subject line and add an explanatory content line at the beginning of the email, before the forward, explaining why one has chosen to forward the email or forward.

- **Clear unwanted information**
  Unwanted information, like the earlier correspondence, that automatically appears if one were to respond by pressing the reply/reply all button, needs to be deleted, before a reply is sent. This helps in reducing clutter as well as prevents making the email unnecessarily heavy. So too, if one is forwarding an email, often the >>>>>>>> signs appear. These can be highly distracting and can reflect a casual attitude to the email as well as towards the receiver and should therefore be cleared, while composing a forward.

- **No short forms**
  Using short forms, instead of fully spelt words, abbreviations or acronyms, makes people believe that they are saving time in email drafting. However, it can result in both miscommunication and ambiguity, defeating the very purpose of communication. Moreover, across generations and cultures, the same acronyms can have different interpretations, resulting in miscommunication. Therefore, while it is fair to use acronyms that appear in the dictionary like PTO (which will not have any relevance in the email context), one should not use others that one may find commonsensical but may not in fact be so (like LOL, while the older generation uses this for Lots of Love, the younger generation means Laugh out Loud, when they refer to it).

- **Paying attention to spellings and grammar**
  While some service providers, like Gmail, offer an in-built spell-check mechanism, others may not do so. However, that cannot excuse spelling or grammatical mistakes, as these can create a poor impression or then result in miscommunication. For e.g. Instead of typing 'Please expect my presence' if one were to type 'Please except my presence' or 'Please expect my presents', the result could be disastrous, with only oneself to blame . While the former would result in the sender being excluded from a function that has an RSVP requirement, the latter could cause disappointment in a receiver, who would be left expecting presents that were nonexistent.

  In order to alleviate this issue, in case the service provider does not offer an in-built spell-check, one can resort to the simple solution of typing the content in Microsoft Word, which offers spell-check, and then pasting it in the email. Often enough, even re-reading the email after having drafted it carefully, though it may appear to be a waste of time or may seem boring to most, can help in getting rid of most spelling and grammatical errors that may have occurred, due to fast typing, attempting to multitask, trying to keep pace with one's thoughts or ones that occur, due to a break in thought, resulting from a variety of reasons.

- **Choice of vocabulary**

  One needs to remember, at all times that the essential purpose of an email is to communicate and not impress. Therefore, one needs to be clearly aware of the recipient(s) and choose one's vocabulary accordingly. For example, instead of using 'Apropos our conversation', one could state, 'As per our discussion', to facilitate understanding. While the former phrase may create a favourable impression about one's vocabulary, it would not help, if the intended recipient does not get the gist of what one desires to state. It makes little sense to expect the intended recipient of the email to refer to a dictionary, to understand what one is attempting to say, through an email.

- **Refrain from one-liners**

  Do not send emails with one-liners/one word, like 'Thanks' 'Ok' etc., in a formal context. This can serve as a response only in the context of family and friends. A formal email has to include a salutation, a sign off line and the proper context of the response.

- **Using exclamation marks/emoticons**

  Often people use exclamation marks to highlight the importance of the matter one is communicating. While primarily this is grammatically incorrect, as the exclamation mark is used as a punctuation, to denote surprise or mark words/sentence that have an emotion embedded in them, in an email using unnecessary as well as too many exclamation marks is also considered rude. If one needs to emphasis on the importance of a particular email that one has sent, it could either begin with the words IMP: in the subject to draw attention to it, or could be followed up with a phone call or an sms.

On the other hand, emoticons, used to reflect emotions that may be difficult to capture in words, are a strict no-no in formal communication, though they can be used in emails between friends/family.

- **Creating a professional sounding email id**
  Often people possess email ids much before they join the professional space. As a result, these email ids have in most cases a very frivolous or comical ring to them. They may often be created in a manner to sound trendy. However, this is not what works or is acceptable in an official environment. It may create in the mind of the receiver an image of the sender as a very casual or immature person at the least or in the worst scenario may lead to the receiver not being able to associate the id with the person who has sent it. For e.g. itsmesachin@rediffmail.com or cutedaisy@gmail.com can result in a lot of unpleasantness if someone takes it upon them to be cheeky and states 'I too am Sachin, you are not the only one' or 'I really don't find you cute at all'.

  An exception to this, though not necessarily so, can be people in the creative field, who often try to explain away things as a reflection of their creative genius. The ideal email id should contain the name and surname in some form and the year of birth or initials, in case the name-surname combination id is not available.

- **Do not use the company email id for personal use**
  Over and above leading to a great deal of embarrassment or inviting strict action, if the id is watched, accessed or hacked, using a company email id for personal reasons is neither ethical nor particularly sensible, if one understands the value of keeping one's personal and professional space apart. It is also necessary to understand that most companies have a backend access to the company email ids of their employees and the employees can therefore be very easily caught, if one is using it to send 'improper'/'confidential' information . So too, an id can be used to archive or save important information; and so, if one leaves the organisation or is asked to leave it, one would either risk losing this information or then would have to spend a lot of time re-sending it to one's personal id, as one would have to give up the official id, when one leaves the organisation. In this light, it is most important to note that using one's professional email id or designation for sending out a job application is a strict no-no.

- **Avoid unnecessarily long emails**
  Although, in an attempt to be cogent, one often writes long emails trying to explain the matter in detail, it is important to realise that an email ought to be concise

and precise to have an impact. Long emails can result in getting greater ambiguity into the matter, can make the reader lose focus, thus missing out on the essence of the communication, or be considered a waste of time by the receiver and may therefore be skimmed over or ignored. Moreover, the actual purpose may get shrouded, in the clutter of information. Thus, emails need to be not only precise and short, but can also highlight important information, like the day/date, time and venue (if included), in a list form, rather than as running matter, in the form of a paragraph.

- **Do not send angry/abusive/aggressive email**
  Emails remain as a written proof, with the receiver of the email; unlike telephonic conversations, made at the spur of the moment. Thus, while very rarely telephonic conversations would get recorded, even if they are abusive, since the listener is caught unaware and therefore does not record it, emails would appear as written proof and can thus be used to file a case of defamation against an individual or the organisation that the individual represents. Moreover, momentary anger cannot be used as an excuse in an email, as one could in a telephonic conversation, since one has enough time to draft and edit it, emails being a mode of written communication. Finally, the receiver too gets adequate time to respond to it and carefully frame what s/he is composing as a reply, so the sender needs to be very careful in the composition of the email. Even if the other person is in the wrong, the sender of the email needs to

word his/her email carefully, so as to reflect a firm displeasure, without being angry, abusive or aggressive.

- **Do not reveal sensitive information in an email**
  Sensitive information, whether personal or professional, should preferably not be revealed via email. The reasons for this can be many. For one, one does not know whether the email id of the receiver is used only by him/her or is serving as a team id or is being accessed by the secretary of the individual to whom the email is sent. In case it is either of the latter, the information may get into hands that one may not want it to. Secondly, one's account may get hacked at any point of time and this sensitive information may fall in the wrong hands and may get liable to be misused. Finally, since email is a written mode of correspondence, if one is revealing sensitive information that should not be divulged, but one is nevertheless sharing with another, the email could serve as a written proof of one's disloyalty/not honouring the boundaries of personal/professional relations.

- **Spell the receiver(s)'s name correctly**
  Getting the receiver's name wrong is not merely careless, but also rude, and can at times result in the email being sent to the wrong receiver or bouncing. So too, since people are fairly attached to their names, since they constitute for the person his/her identity, basic courtesy demands that one should respect this, since one wishes to establish connection with the person.

- **Utilise Cc and Bcc effectively**
  While Cc is marked to all those who are to be informed but need not act on an issue; Bcc is meant for those who need to be in the loop, but without the others in the email having knowledge of it. Not realising this, people at times forward emails to those whom they want to include in the Bcc. However, this is a waste of the sender's time. So too, if the individual(s) is included in 'To' instead of 'Cc', s/he may be wrongly led to believe that s/he is expected to act on it and may get confused as a result. Also, one need not fear/ needs to be aware that the reply to the email will not reach the person, who has been included in the Bcc. However, all those included in the Cc will receive the reply, if one hits the 'Reply All' button.

  It is also important to note that at times while 'To:' is used for those who are responsible for action, 'Cc:' is used for escalation of the matter under consideration, if one has been trying to get an issue addressed and the receiver is not responding to it.

- **Using 'Reply' or 'Reply All'**
  One needs to be conscious and cautious, while replying to an email, as hitting the 'Reply All' button, instead of 'Reply', can prove to be both inconvenient, as those not concerned with the reply would have their inboxes flooded with unwanted mail, and embarrassing, as people may become privy to information that one may

not necessarily wish to share with them. While 'Reply is meant to respond to only the person, who has sent the email, 'Reply All' would go to all the individuals included in the email chain, whether they are marked in 'To' or in 'CC'; however the reply would not go to those, who have been included in 'Bcc'.

- **Subject line**

  Ambiguous subject lines or emails sent without including any subject line whatsoever can lead to the email not getting the attention/ serious thought it deserves. It is therefore necessary to see that the subject line used is indicative of the content of the email and expectation of the sender. Moreover, it is important that the subject line should be short, as long subject lines defeat their very purpose. It is worth noting that the subject line appears even before opening the email, as a part of the inbox. Therefore, the receiver presumes the content of the email and may process it/ value it accordingly. Non inclusion of subject lines or ambiguous subject lines could also make the receiver believe that the email contains spam. In fact, at times, even the default spam filter of the service provider would recognise such emails as spam and not deliver them to the receiver or make them appear in the receiver's spam folder.

- **No random sign-off line**

  An email is different from a letter and therefore 'Yours sincerely/faithfully' is not an appropriate sign off line. Similarly 'Cheers'/'Ciao' are extremely casual and cannot be used in formal/semi formal emails. So too, except in organisations related to the U.S. 'Thanks and Regards' often do not go together, as the word 'Thanks' has an informal ring to it, while 'Regards' is a term of respect. More so, not including a sign off line at all makes the email sound abrupt and lacking in professional decency. An acceptable line to sign off with in all formal emails is 'Regards' or 'Warm Regards', in case the relationship with the receiver is one that has been built over time.

- **Attachments**

  Attachments should be sent only when necessary, as they take time to view or download and should be saved in a lower version, so that they can be easily accessed or opened by the receiver, who may not necessarily have access to the higher version of a software. Latest versions should in fact be avoided to the maximum extent possible, although they may make one feel very tech-savvy.

  Often, people repeat in attachments, what they have already stated in the email. This is because they believe that the attachment, which is often a signed and scanned copy, serves as an authoritative proof of what is said in the email. In such cases, rather than repeating matter, it is better to put in the content of the email 'Please find attached, my/the note on ..... for your perusal and action'. What may otherwise happen is that people may stop opening the attachments, as they would find it a waste of time and may, as a result, miss out on the content of the attachment, if it is something different from the content of the email.

Most importantly, the name given to the attachment should be indicative and representative rather than being merely functional. The title 'Exam paper 2013 in Communication for Part Time students' though long is more accurate than just 'Exam paper'.

- **Know when to or when not to reply**

  Replying because you have nothing better to do or because you believe that courtesy demands it can result in a great deal of inconvenience to the receiver, by uselessly occupying his/her time and space in his/her inbox. More so, the person may be left wondering, why you have replied, making him/her bemused or creating a suspicion in his/her mind.

  On the other hand, not replying to an email, where a reply is expected, can show a casual attitude or may result in misunderstanding. Therefore, it is important to carefully reflect on the content of an email, before deciding whether or not to reply to it.

- **Know when to call**
  It may not always be sensible to send an email or to respond to an email with an email. It may be at times important to call instead. One needs to be aware of this and make an accurate decision, if one needs to send an email or call. So too, if the issue is extremely urgent, one may have to send an email and follow it up immediately with a call (since very few persons are constantly logged in), only call or only send an sms (as the person may be travelling and may not have email access).

  For example, it is better to call, if one has got the contact of another from a third person and one wishes to invite this person as a Chief Guest. At such times, it is better to call the person before randomly dashing of an email and after having spoken to him/her, one can follow it up with an email.

- **Seek permission for daily message lists**
  Some messages like daily reports or feel-good initiatives, like birthday greetings, thoughts for the day, commendation for services or season's greetings, are sent in certain organisations. However, these can again prove to be space blockers or time-wasters for people, who are travelling, are extremely busy or have their emails checked by their secretaries. In this context, it is important that one seeks the permission of the person(s) whom one wishes to include in this list.

- **Manner of responding to chat when busy**
  One may have enabled chat on one's email, to facilitate communication, especially since it proves to be faster and can be used to communicate about minor things, with intra or inter organisational colleagues and friends. However, at times, one may be busy, when the chat window pops up in one's email account, which is open for some other purpose. At such times, miscommunication can result, if one ignores the chat or randomly logs out of the email, because one is busy and does not have the time to chat. At such times, it is advisable to either reply to the person that one is busy and won't be able to chat or if one is not active on the email and sees the pop up much later, it is important to write a line apologising for missing out on the person's chat, since, though one has logged in, one is at that moment not active on the email account.

The purpose of any communication is to get across what one wishes to and minimise any barriers that may hinder communication or may result in miscommunication. A simple way to enhance and ensure the effectiveness of an email is following etiquette, which though it may evolve with time and culture, basically remains the same.

Common Errors in Drafting emails

Emails form an important part of office communication, both internal and external. In fact, some offices, in order to do away with wastage and filing of paper, as also in order to reduce expenses, rely totally on emails for communication; since they offer the convenience of the written word, while serving a legal purpose, as they can be stored and produced as evidence, in case of a dispute. However, despite their convenience, if errors in emails are not avoided, at the least they can lead to miscommunication or show the sender in a poor light; but at worse, they can create hassles, for either the sender or the receiver.

Most of these errors can be avoided, by being aware or taking extra care, in using emails, as a form of communication.

- **Subject Lines**
  It is important to understand that the subject line is a necessary and important part of every email. This is because the subject line appears as an indicator in the inbox, even before one opens an email. Therefore, the absence of a subject line can reduce the importance of an email. Moreover, service providers like Gmail offer direct screening benefits, such as marking an email important, based on either the sender or the subject line. Therefore, it is absolutely vital to include a subject line, in every email.

Additionally, the subject line of an email needs to be indicative and precise. Long subject lines create redundancy, whereas an unclear subject line would serve to have no additional value. In fact it may mislead the receiver into believing that the email is on some other matter, therefore reducing its priority for him/her. So too, certain top authorities, especially of the old school rely on secretaries, to scan their email. A vague subject line would mean that the secretary does not bring the email to the notice of his/her boss.

In this context, it is worth noting that while forwarding an email, the word 'forward' (Fwd) automatically appears in the subject line. This naturally reduces its importance. To prevent this from happening, one needs to remove the word forward (Fwd) and/or redraft the subject line, to cover the context to which one wishes to draw the attention of the receiver. The sender can then compose his/her message and send the forward as an attachment or text, following the sender's email. For example, if one is forwarding a leave application to the HR, it is better to change the subject line to *Leave Application of Mr. Satyen Pinge* rather than leaving it as *Fwd: My Leave Application*.

- **Improper and informal salutation**
  Some very common modes of salutation, used even in formal emails, are *Hi!, Hey*! or *Dear All*. However, all these are inappropriate for different reasons. While the first two are very casual/ informal and therefore do not

befit a formal email and would also clash with the tone of the content, making it lose its seriousness; the other (*Dear All*) is incorrect. One can use *Dear Mr./Ms. First Name or Surname* depending upon the etiquette followed in the organisation to which one belongs, the country of one's origin or the relationship shared with the receiver of the email. More so, one could also use just the first name, without the title Mr./Ms., if one is writing to a professional friend/junior. Similarly, *Dear All* can be replaced with either *Dear Colleagues* or *Dear Team Members*. 'Colleagues' is a term that includes people at the same level as well as those who are senior or junior. However, due caution must be exercised, while spelling the word 'colleagues'.

- **Tone of the Message**

  All official email is of necessity formal. One should therefore maintain an appropriate tone, while drafting such an email. Often, people draft emails, as if they are holding a casual conversation with the other person. This is not acceptable, as per email etiquette. Moreover, use of slang and colloquialisms should also be avoided, while drafting an email.

  It is important to realise that there is no non-verbal communication available, to supplement what one is saying in an email. So too, one has enough time to draft, edit and check the draft of an email before sending it. A poor tone therefore becomes unacceptable. For example, instead of *See Ya* one could use *Hoping to see you* or

Looking forward to seeing you, depending upon the level of formality one wishes to bring in.

While small letters are considered acceptable in emails, where one is corresponding with those one is regularly in touch with in formal situations, using all caps i.e. all capital letters is a complete no-no. If one needs to draw attention, one can make a couple of words/sentences bold or formulate the content in such a way as to draw attention to certain information. All capital letters are considered equivalent to 'shouting', while speaking, and therefore cannot be a part of formal official communication.

- **Use of short forms**

  Short forms like *PFA* or *FYI* though in common use are not terms that are universally understood, whether across ages or cultures. For example, while some members of an older generation believe *Lol* to be *Lots of Love*, most of the younger generation consider it to be *laugh out loud.* This can definitely create a great deal of miscommunication and misinterpretation. Moreover, these acronyms are not listed in the dictionary and are therefore not a part of standardised vocabulary. So also, some of them may be highly contextual and used with a very specific reference point, like TGIF – Thank God It's Friday, which is used both for a dressing line and as the name of a restaurant chain.

Usually, people use short forms, in order to save time, in the context of common actions, like those of sending attachments. This is a legitimate concern and a hurdle, which could be overcome by keeping a template of the commonly used phrases available on a word document, on one's computer.

- **Ambiguity**

  Generic words that indicate time, place, people etc. should be avoided in an email, as the email might be accessed at a later point in time and the person may not see the date and time, when it has been sent/delivered. So too, the delivery of the email may be delayed, due to a variety of technical reasons, making generic words ambiguous, thus making the communication ineffective, with the fault being laid at the door of the sender.

  Words, like - as decided earlier, yesterday, tomorrow, here, there or pronouns like he/she, him/ her, should be used carefully. For example, he told her to meet him at the same place tomorrow may mean nothing to the receiver or could cause immense confusion' if the person means Ram told Sita to meet Lakshman at Thane on Saturday, 16th February, 2013 at 5.00 pm.

- **Choice of vocabulary**

  Words that may sound good may not necessarily convey the meaning, one desires them to. It is therefore important to be aware of the audience, while choosing the words that one would use to communicate. For example, *apropos our discussion,* though correct, may not make the meaning evident to a person, who is not very fluent in English; in such a case it might be better to use the more easily understood *as per our discussion* or *further to our discussion.*

- **Sending an attachment in the higher version/not in the compatible mode**
  One is not aware of the operating system of the receiver. Therefore, it is always sensible to send an attachment in a lower version; since, if the receiver possesses a lower version operating system than the sender, an attachment, despite being properly attached, would not open on the receiver's computer. For example, most people send attachments in the .docx form i.e. a word document saved in the Microsoft Office 2007 version. However, some organisations still use the Microsoft 2003 version. Thus, an email sent in a higher version would not open on the receiver's computer. Moreover, some individuals find it trendy to show their accessibility to latest technology and therefore use the latest technology that is on offer. However, it is important to note that suitability and convenience are of greater essence than showing how technologically- savvy one is.

- **Unusual formats**
  Information technology being an evolving field, there are constant innovations and changes being brought about,

in existing formats as well as the creation of new ones. Often, those not directly in touch with the information technology field or those not particularly computer savvy are not able to keep abreast with these changing developments. Therefore, if an attachment is sent in the latest format, the receiver may not know how to access it. In fact, in India though most using computers are familiar with 'Word', few know how to use 'Excel' or even view hyperlinked elements in PPTs.

- **Non-indicative file names**
  Often file names are given, using short forms, dates or even generic terms, like resume. This can lead to a great deal of confusion, in saving as well as accessing files. For example, if more than twenty candidates have applied for a job and most of them have named their curriculum vitae files 'Resume', the person reading it may use that as a point for elimination, during short-listing the candidates for an interview.

- **Not following etiquette/ protocol**
  Like all forms of communication (whether oral, written or non-verbal), emails too have their own etiquette/protocol. However, these are not often specified or written down in the manner of a rule book; yet their violation/ignorance about these can result in issues, ranging from creating a bad impression to causing

miscommunication. It is therefore important to be conscious of the etiquette to be followed, while sending an email. While some aspects of the etiquette change from one organisation and one culture to another, as well as over time, certain other aspects remain common. Thus, while in an MNC, with its head office in America, it may be acceptable to use American spellings, using all capital letters is not acceptable, whichever the organisation/location. Similarly, unparliamentary language or abusive words violate email etiquette and can land the sender in legal complications.

- **Sending the email without checking it**

  In a hurry, individuals often send emails without checking the content for spelling, grammar or even matter. This is totally unacceptable, as it displays a casual attitude/ negligence, on the part of the sender. In the odd event that such a thing occurs, despite the care one may exercise, it is important to resend the email, beginning with a clear apology for one's oversight.

  In the context of matter, oversight can include forgetting to add a subject line, forgetting to send attachments, sending the wrong email to a person, not marking a person as Cc: or as an additional receiver in the To: line, including the wrong person in an email or sending an email to the wrong id (in case people have separate personal and professional ids).

To avoid such an error from occurring, it is best to add the sender ('To:') last in an email - after the email is drafted, edited and verified. This will prevent the email from being sent, even if one hits the send button, by mistake.

- **Sending professional emails on personal ids and vice versa**
  Often people have separate ids for their personal and professional work. It is possible that one may have access to both, if one shares more than a casual acquaintance with a person. One should in such cases be careful that one does not send the content to the wrong id, as the mail may either get ignored, not get attention within the required time or may be accessed by the wrong person.
  At times, secretaries or even team members have access to their boss's/colleague's professional email account. This would mean that some information/comment or forward, sent in a light vein, may be accessed by a person, who should not be viewing it, creating awkwardness, both for the intended receiver and the person who reads it.

  Moreover, if professional email gets sent to a personal id, the account may not get accessed, if a person is travelling or extremely busy at the workplace and therefore a delay in time in accessing the email could create an issue, like loss of validity of the content. So too, the value of the email would get reduced, if it is sent on the personal id, as the individual accessing it may not register the content and act upon it, if one is caught up in a busy schedule.

In order to make emails effective and ensure that they have the desired impact upon the receiver, it is thus important to ensure that errors are minimised, if not totally eradicated, by taking note of the issues that repeatedly occur in emails, making them less effective.

Managing emails

Emails have become such an important aspect of day-to-day written communication that both on a professional and a personal level, individuals receive a lot of emails. As a result, if the emails are allowed to accumulate, they can create a lot of clutter, making one miss out on important information. So too, if one spends far too much time, accessing or replying to one's emails, one's day-to-day routine work, at office/home, can suffer immensely, leading to a vicious circle of piling up and generating a backlog.

Moreover, emails also serve a legal purpose, in case a dispute arises between individuals or organisations. Therefore, it is important to save emails that one may have to produce as legal proof. Additionally, since emails can be accessed from anywhere and serve to reduce the accumulation of paper, they need to be used and managed efficiently, so as to make them work for you, without proving to be a hindrance/nuisance.

- **Viewing**

  Checking emails becomes an obsession with most. People are either logged into their email accounts all day long or then keep checking their emails very frequently, often at the frequency of every 15 minutes to half-an-hour. While the former can lead to security issues, making your account easy to access or hack; both the former and the latter can result in a great deal of distraction and wastage of time. On the other hand, not checking emails at a regular interval may lead to the information being received becoming outdated and therefore irrelevant as also missing out on important communication, like intimations about meetings etc.

Emails thus need to be accessed at a frequency that is conducive, but not debilitating. One can thus access them immediately after arriving in office; pre or post lunch and once prior to leaving the office. This helps, since when one checks the email immediately on coming to work, one can access all emails that may have come after one has left office and can thus help in planning out one's day. The pre or post lunch and before leaving checking session would on the other hand help in acting upon mails that may be arriving, as the working day proceeds and may highlight what others may require of you, as the day unfolds; moreover, the latter would help ensuring that there is not much left pending for the next day, so that one can being afresh, with only whatever has come in after one has left, appearing as unread in the inbox.

However, some believe that it does not make sense to check the emails first thing on coming to work, as this is a quiet time, you can spend, as per what you have planned out, and an email can entirely change the course of this plan. Emails thus need to be accessed as per what one finds convenient; what one needs to remember though is that, accessing emails should not result in inconvenience either to the sender or receiver and should follow a plan and not be random.

- **Archiving**

  Certain emails need to be preserved for eternity or at least for a given span of time, as they may contain information that may have legal implications, for the individual or the organisation. So too, they have some relevance for a particular span of time, since they may be required for reference or action. Keeping these emails in the inbox may result in unnecessarily cluttering the inbox, causing nuisance for oneself, may slow down email access or may even result in the inbox being full (depending upon the capacity offered by the service provider). It thus becomes important to archive them, by clicking on the archive feature, which appears as a tab option; this results in the email being saved as an archive, which one can retrieve as often as possible, de-cluttering of the inbox and affording access as often and for as long as one may require.

- **Mark as Important/ Add star**

  A facility provided by some service providers, one can add a star to an email (and remove it at any point one desires) to draw attention towards it, from among the numerous unread emails that may be lying in one's inbox. Moreover, depending upon the sender (the frequency with which s/he sends the receiver an email) and/or key words in an email, the in-built filter of an email inbox can mark an email as important, to draw one's attention to it. However, this facility is not made available by all service providers.

- **Save Drafts**

  Content or replies that may need to be used often can be saved as templates, under drafts. This helps in saving a lot of time and helps in reducing repetitive work. So too, certain content/replies that need to be sent at a later point can be created and saved under drafts, when one has the free time, so that one can save time, when one has to actually send the email and one might be busy. Drafts can also constitute ideas that have crossed one's mind or greetings, whose time has not come, but which, if not jotted down, may be forgotten, in the routine of one's working day.

- **Signature**

  The signature line (i.e. name, designation and company name and, depending upon company protocol, the company logo and tagline) can be saved to appear as default signature, in the company email id that one may be using, since it is required at the end of every email; and if it appears by default, it would save a lot of time and prevent repetitive work. However, if on an odd occasion, one were to use this email id, to send personal/semiformal emails, one should ensure that one edits the signature line; else it could result in misunderstanding.

- **Mark as unread**

Despite reading one's email, one can mark it as unread, if one desires to return to it, either in order to reply to it later or refer to it again.

- **Creating Labels**

  Certain service providers offer the option of creating varied folders, under the headings 'labels', so as to categorise the emails, depending upon the sender/content of the email. This helps in organising the inbox and making accessibility simple and convenient, in order to retrieve/refer to existent emails. The varied labels available are 'personal' – for family and friends' emails; 'receipts' – for electronically generated/scanned receipts, bank statements etc.; 'travel' – for travel itinerary and e-tickets etc.; 'work' – official; create new – this gives one the freedom to create labels as per one's choice.

- **Move to a specific folder**

  To organise one's emails, one has the option of creating labels (personal, receipts, travel, work) and grouping existent emails under these heads or moving them to the 'spam' (if suspicious) or 'trash' (if unwanted) folders.

- **Emptying Trash**

  It is essential to empty trash, at frequent intervals. This is because trash too occupies space and can reduce the space available for other folders; so also, not all service providers offer the facility of 'emptying the trash' after a certain time span elapses (e.g. 30 days in Gmail). More importantly, any confidential email that one may delete gets stored in trash; and if one's account is hacked, it can be accessed; in these circumstances, it is more valuable to delete this email from the trash folder as well. One also has the option of emptying trash, by selecting and deleting one email at a time, from the trash box, or pressing 'select all/purge', thereby getting rid of all emails in the trash box, at the same time.

- **Spam – not replying and cleaning**

  Spam i.e. emails which have suspicious senders/subjects can contain virus that may harm the computer; even otherwise, they add no value and would only result in wastage of time, if one were to read them. Moreover, accumulated spam is deleted, after a time span, by certain service providers, till then, it merely occupies space. Spam can also appear as quarantined matter in the inbox, based on the facilities offered by the service provider and can be released, by using a password that appears within the 'marked' email, since the marking is done by the service provider. What one needs to remember is that one should, under no circumstances, reply to 'spam' and should preferably delete it regularly, to reduce clutter.

- **Deleting read mails**

Once an email has been read, it is important to delete it immediately, if one has no future legal or reference use for it. If this is not done, double the time is wasted, accessing it again, merely to decide to delete it; else, piled up emails can unnecessarily block available inbox space.

- **Out of station automated reply**

  Certain service providers offer the scope to set an out of station automated reply. If and when activated, it sends out a pre-set reply to all those, who have sent one an email that one is 'out of office', till such and such a date. This helps prevent misunderstanding, if one does not reply to an email received at such a time and also gives the person, sending an email, the option of contacting you, using some other channel of communication, if the matter is extremely important. Moreover, one can customise the 'out of office' reply message, to include details like one's date of return or whom/where to contact during one's absence.

- **Mute**

  Emails that are marked mute are not reflected in the inbox window, though they appear there. Thus, a confidential email that needs to be stored can be marked 'mute', as, even if one's email account is hacked or accessed by a colleague, the 'mute' email will not be reflected there. One can key in the name of the sender, whose email one has made 'mute', in the search box, after opening the inbox page, the email then becomes visible and can be accessed or removed from the 'mute' status.

- **Searching**

  One can search for any email that one has received and is either in one's inbox, sent or trash, using the search option. For this, one can type the sender's name, email id or key content words, in the search box and a list of related emails appears. So also, one can search emails that one has made 'mute', using this option.

- **Activating the address book**

  Activating the address book/updating the contact list helps preserve all the details of the person's contact and can fulfil the purpose of what was earlier called phonebook/diary or later called the electronic diary. Moreover, the contacts in the address book/contact list can be categorised and organised in a way, so as to facilitate convenience. Additionally, this address book/contact list can be accessed from anywhere, at any time, using any device that provides one an access to one's email.

- **Account sync**

  One can sync one's email account with one's tablet/mobile phone and keep receiving and checking the emails, while on the move, which will make it not merely convenient, but also easily accessible and can help in saving office time, if one checks one's emails, while travelling.

- **Organisational policies**

  How often one can access emails and more importantly how many emails can be stored and whether or not all internal organisational correspondence can take place through emails would depend upon organisational policies. It is thus important that organisations have fair/acceptable policies, in this regard. Also, if this is not so, it is important for employees, to attempt to address the issues, for the wellbeing of both the individual and the organisation.

Managing emails well not only enhances the value of the medium, but also helps increase one's productivity and efficiency. What is more important to remember though is that the converse is also true. This implies that if one does not utilise the medium well, it could not only prove cumbersome but also disastrous, defeating the very purpose of the medium.

Email Specimens

Forward: As itself

Subject: Information on MISTCON 2012 for the website

From: feliciar_mi@au.edu

Date: Fri, April 6, 2012 4:36 pm

To: ankushd_mi@au.edu

Dear Ankush

As discussed, find the details of the conference attended by Parikshit Vyavhare – Faculty, Media Management, for your perusal and action.

Regards
Felicia Rogers
Associate Professor, Communication
Ambika University

--------------------------- Original Message ---------------------------
Subject: MISTCON 2012
From: parikshit_mi@au.edu
Sent: Fri, April 6, 2012 12:42 pm
To: feliciar_mi@au.edu

Mam

As discussed this morning, please find attached the documents of the International Conference, in which I had presented a Poster.

I have discussed the matter with Prof. Pinto and he has asked me to send a copy to you for our website; thus I am sending across a soft copy.

Regards
Parikshit Vyavhare
Assistant Professor, Media Management
Ambika University

Forward: As an attachment

Subject: Need for Research Associate
From: rutujaf_ncrsai@bsu.edu
Date: Fri, January 4, 2013 1:24 pm
To: anitaj_ncrsai@bsu.edu, latikan_ncrsai@bsu.edu, mrudulap_ncrsai@bsu.edu
Attachment: Application 1KB
CV 2KB

Dear Mam/Latika/Mrudula

As per our discussion yesterday, find attached the email and CV of Ms Madhushree Bhagwat for the post of Research Associate. Since she possesses the qualifications I require, it would be immensely beneficial for me to have her in my team.

Many thanks,

Regards
Rutuja Fatarfekar
Professor, International Business
BSU NCRSAI

Requesting: Inviting

Subject: Invitation as an Expert
From: pujat.ims@nimm.edu
Date: Wed, August 10, 2011 1:24 pm
To: aniket@gmail.com

Dear Aniket

NIMM's Institute of Media Studies is conducting a training programme, for students, in effectively drafting and presenting their thoughts on 'My Role as a Media Professional' and 'Media Ethics'. Though I would be providing the inputs, we wish to have with us a panel of experts, from the academia and industry, to guide and assess the students; since the training is being conducted in the workshop mode.

We would be extremely privileged, if you accede to our request, to serve as an expert on the panel, on Saturday, 20th August, 2011 and Wednesday, 24th August, 2011, from 9.00 am to 6.00 pm. The training will be conducted at our Bindu Nagar Campus, behind Humayun Hospital. Over and above the breakfast, lunch and evening tea, which will be on the house, we offer our experts a modest honorarium of Rs.1000 per hour.

Do revert to me on 9969423122, in case of any further queries. We look forward to having you with us, on both these days.

Regards
Puja Thakur
Associate Professor, Media Studies
NIMM's I

Requesting: Approval

Subject: Invitation as an Expert
From: pervezb.udom@pet.edu
Date: Thu, September 30, 2010 1:24 pm
To: mihirs.udom@pet.edu
Cc: manishs.udom@pet.edu
Bcc: mitikaj.udom@pet.edu

Dear Sir

As per our discussion this evening, I request you to confirm on Monday, 4th October, 2010, when we could host Mr. Shree Savera from Yuhu University, in order to establish ties internationally, as we are desirous of doing. As was mentioned to you during our conversation, he is here from 25th to 27th October, 2010 and can address our students on Marketing Strategies, which is his forte.

This would also give us an opportunity to discuss long term tie ups with Yuhu for academic exchange.

Could you kindly revert by Monday, so that we do not miss this opportunity, as he may be tied up with various other activities while he is here?

Regards
Pervez Bhoj
Dy. General Manager, Liaison
PET

Requesting: Action

Subject: Request to book the Guest House
From: priyashirpurkar.ls@mrvs.edu
Date: Tue, February 26, 2013 11:51 am
To: veenam@nbia.in

Dear Madam

I would be travelling to Kolhapur on 8th March, 2013, to deliver a talk at AIWEC on Women's Empowerment. To facilitate reaching there on time, I request you to book an accommodation for me and Manisha Gadiwala, who would be travelling with me, on 7th and 8th March 2013, at the NBIA Pune campus Guest House.

If I reach Pune at a reasonable hour in the evening, after the talk, I would however like to proceed towards Mumbai on the same evening i.e. 8th March, 2013. The reservation of the accommodation for both the days would however save me a great deal of inconvenience. Moreover, in case you wish to discuss the research journal issue, we could try and meet up at 4.30 pm on 7th March, 2013, since I would be in Pune anyway.

Please do let me know, so that I could carry the relevant papers. Many thanks for your continuous and prompt support,

Warm regards
Priya Shipurkar
Associate Professor, Language Studies
MRVS Institute

Responding

Subject: Classroom for Sessions in Communication
From: priyashirpurkar.ls@mrvs.edu
Date: Wed, December 12, 2012 10:15 am
To: sridharr@mrvs.edu

Dear Sridhar

Received your email about the 24th. I would, as accepted earlier, be conducting sessions for the Junior MCA students, every Monday and Thursday from 11.30 am to 1.30 pm beginning 24th December, 2012. Could you however kindly confirm the classroom?

Regards
Priya Shirpurkar
Associate Professor, Language Studies
MRVS Institute

Informing

Specimen 1

Subject: Change in EDUFUN date
From: vinayakpadwal.dir@or.edu
Date: Mon, August 8, 2011 1:24 pm
To: cchikhale@savewater.org

Dear Mr Chikhale

Thank you for having consented to deliver a talk on Water Conservation at our annual cultural event – OR EDUFUN. The date of the event, however, has now been changed, due to unavoidable circumstances. The planning of the event is underway and as soon as the agenda is firmed up, we would revert to you and share the details of the programme with you.

We hope that you would be able to spare the time, to share your views, with the staff and students of the Institute, as it would be an honour to have you amongst us. We regret the inconvenience caused and thank you for your cooperation.

Regards
Prof. Vinayak Padwal
Director
RM Mandali's OR League of Colleges

Informing
Specimen 2

Subject: Exemption from the Part Time exam
From: sunitap.sm@or.edu
Date: Sat, March 3, 2012 4:16 pm
To: sandeshg.fm@or.edu, nirmank.fm@or.edu

Dear Sandesh/Nirman

As per my discussion with Nawale Sir, the following faculty members would not be available for participating in conducting the GD/PI for Part Time entrance exams, to be held on 9th March, 2012, since we are attending the workshop Unboggle the Blog, on the same day.

Dr. Fatima Qureshi
Ramesh Phaterphekar
Vaikunth Paradkar
Malvika Naik
Dr. Sunita Pandit
Regret the inconvenience caused and thank you for your understanding,

Regards
Sunita Pandit
Professor, Strategic Management
RM Mandali's OR League of Colleges

Apologising

Subject: Apology for not sending you the word-a-day
From: minakshis.css@inc.edu
Date: Mon, December 3, 2012 9.36 am
To: amitg.nm@inc.edu

Dear Amit

In all the mess related to teaching across institutes currently, I must admit that I completely forgot what you had asked of me. So, first let me apologise for the lapse on my part, which I shall address with immediate effect.

As far as I remember, you had asked me to send you a new word each day. Is that correct? If not, please remind me about what was it that you wanted me to do and I shall work on it.

Sorry for the delay once again.

Regards
Minakshi Sunderesan
Associate Professor, Language and Literature
INC CSS

Thanking

Connecting

Subject: Request for mentoring and coaching students

From: swatinagarkatti.liaison@srti.edu

Date: Fri, March 8, 2013 10:16 am

To: riteshd@gmail.com,manoj-r@rediffmail.com,purnima.bhaskaran@hotmail.com, supriyawalawalkar@yahoo.com

Dear Alumni

For the last 24 years, Suryoday Research and Training Institute has been striving to deliver quality education, a journey which has so far been fruitful and possible, due to the relentless support that you have offered us.

In an attempt to foster a greater idea exchange between the students on campus and you, as professionals, we would like to establish a platform which could facilitate mentoring and coaching of students. The emotional and professional connect that the students feel with you, as has been observed from the varied pre-placement training programmes and the 'Alumni Speak' sessions during *Uday*, go a long way in leaving an impact on the minds of the students. An opportunity to coach and mentor a group of students, in your area of expertise, would help us in making students aware of the realities of the corporate world and equip them with the knowledge of the skills and the domain specific inputs that they lack.

In this light, we request you to register your interest via email by 22nd March, 2013. We also request you to mention a specific domain, in which you could serve as a facilitator, for coaching and mentoring of students. We assure you that the schedule that would be chalked out for this initiative would be flexible and mutually convenient. You will be entitled for privileges of a visiting faculty, covering professional courtesies and access to SRTI academicians. Kindly fill the attached form, if interested.

Looking forward to connecting with you.

Regards

Swati Nagarkatti
Liaison Officer
SRTI

Reporting (daily message chain)

Subject: Website Team Report for 18/07/2012
From: parikshitrao.teamlead@dbrgroup.in
Date: Wed, July 18, 2012 10:19 am
To: punitadarde.hrlead@dbrgroup.in
Cc: viveksalunkhe.ceo@dbrgroup.in

Dear Mam

The project achievement report of our Website Team for 18th July, 2012

Work completed:

Layout

i. A detailed discussion was done for the following pages

   - Home Page
   - Mission and Vision
   - Our Team
   - News and Views
   - Contact us

ii. The two pages, whose designs were complete (as mentioned under the heading Design) were reviewed, and while the one on Suggestions was passed, further improvements in colour and font were suggested for Our Products, as it was appearing very cluttered. It is to be re-reviewed after 2 days.

Design

a. All, other than Ms Sharavari Thakur, Designer, were present. Though Ms Sharavari is not attending, due to a fractured leg, she has completed her part of the page design from home.

b. Two completed pages were sent to the layout team i.e. Suggestions and Our Products

c. Over the next two days we are to work on the suggestions on Our Products and Home Page

Work pending

1. Pages sent by the Layout Team on 18th July. These other than the one mentioned will take a week, as we are working for merely three days next week.

2. Seeking final approval of colour scheme from the CEO, a meeting with whom has been scheduled for 23rd July.

Regards

Parikshit Rao
Team Lead
Website Design and Layout

Office protocol

Subject: Inability to swipe in on 1st April, 2013
From: prathaman-arts@gu.ac.in
Date: Mon, April 1, 2013 10:35am
To: hemantg-peoplesofficer@gu.ac.in
Cc: snigdhas-headarts@gu.ac.in

Dear Hemant

I came in at 9.30 am today (i.e.1st April, 2013), but was unable to swipe in, despite trying for more than 5 minutes. I therefore request you to consider this mail as a verification of my presence at work. Regret the inconvenience. Many thanks.

Regards
Prathama Nambiar
Assistant Professor, History
Faculty of Arts

Office Initiatives

Specimen 1

Subject: Congratulations! Your Contribution Matters
From: rahulraut.teamhr@niecomm.in
Date: Tue, February 5, 2013 10:40 am
To: employees.niecomm@niecomm.in

Dear Colleagues

On behalf of entire NIECOMM Family, we congratulate you on completing memorable years of service with us today...

- 7 years of service: Mr. Suresh Nemane (HR Department)
- 5 years of service: Ms. Ashuti Koregaonkar (Finance Department)

Thanks for being a part of the NIECOMM family.

We are sure that you would continue to put your best foot forward, in the years to come.

With best wishes!

Warm regards

Team HR

Office Initiatives

Specimen 2

Subject: New Year Greetings
From: abubenadhem@bhelandegroup.in
Date: Mon, December 31, 2012 06:00 pm
To: bhelandeteam@bhelandegroup.in

Dear Members of the Bhelande Group

The New Year is a time of great joy: a time for consolidation of past successes, learning from the past failures, planning for the future and marching ahead with great determination.

I wish you the very best for the coming year and hope that it helps you scale ever greater heights. Casting a fleeting glimpse at the year gone by, I would also like to thank you for making the Bhelande Group a great place to work in and assure you that we will all keep working with the same undeterred enthusiasm and passion.

Happy New Year and All the Best

Warm regards

Abu Ben Adhem
CEO, Bhelande Group.

Bibliography

Books

- Dr. ALEX, K (2009): *Soft Skills: Know Yourself & Know the World*, New Delhi: S. Chand & Company Ltd.
- BOOHER, Dianna (2001): *E- Writing: 21st Century Tools for Effective Communication*, Texas USA: Macmillan.
- CHAPMAN, Rebecca, (2007): *English for Emails*, UK: Oxford University Press.
- Dr. JAIN, V. K and Dr. BIYANI, Omprakash (2007): *Business Communication*, New Delhi: S. Chand & Company.
- FLYNN, Nancy (2011): *Keep Your Inbox Under Control*, New Delhi: Axzo Press, Second Edition.
- GOODHUE, Nhu Le, (2011): *Effective Email for the Professional*, USA: CreateSpace Independent Publishing Platform.
- MOHAN, Krishna, BANERJI, Meera (2009): *Developing Communication Skills*, New Delhi: Macmillan.
- O'ROURKE, James, SINGH, Anubha (2006): *Management Communication: A Case-Analysis Approach*, India: Dorling Kindersley (India) Pvt. Ltd.

- SHIRODKAR, Preeti, (2010): *Knowing Your Words' Worth: A Practical Guide To Communicating Effectively in English*, Navi Mumbai: Shroff Publishers and Distributors Pvt. Ltd.

Web sources

- http://brunerbiz.com/email/tips-for-structuring-six-types-of-emails, visited on 26th October, 2012.
- http://ezinearticles.com, visited on 18th October, 2012.
- http://lifehackery.com, visited on 2nd March, 2013.
- http://smallbusiness.chron.com, visited on 18th October, 2012.
- http://web.ebscohost.com, visited on 18th October, 2012.
- www.artofmanliness.com, visited on 20th October, 2012.
- www.buzzle.com, visited on 18th October, 2012.
- www.canyons.edu, visited on 28th March, 2013.
- www.fastcompany.com, visited on 20th March, 2013.
- www.hanyangowl.org, visited on 22nd October, 2012.
- www.inc.com, 5th April, 2013.
- www.indiaparenting.com, visited on 21st October, 2012.
- www.ipc.be, visited on 18th October, 2012
- www.youngentrepreneur.com/blog/12-golden-rules-of-email-etiquette/, visited on 23rd October, 2012.

SHROFF PUBLISHERS & DISTRIBUTORS PVT. LTD.

Shroff Reprints & Original Titles
The X Team Series
(An Imprint of Shroff Publishers)

Computers

ISBN	Title	Author	Year	Price
9789350236321	.NET Interview Q&A, 164 Pages	Harwani	2012	225.00
9789350237830	Advanced Java for Students, 216 Pages	Mehta	2012	250.00
9788184041569	Ajax for Beginners (B/CD), 452 Pages	Bayross	2006	375.00
9788184041972	Application Development with Oracle & PHP on Linux for Beginners, 2/ed (B/CD), 940 Pages	Bayross	2007	650.00
9789351100898	**Artificial Intelligence & Soft Computing for Beginners, 260 Pages**	**Das**	**2013**	**350.00**
9789350233733	Blogging for Beginners, 268 Pages	Harwani	2011	350.00
9788184046397	C for Beginners, 532 Pages	Mothe	2009	400.00
9789350233900	C Interviews Q&A, 192 Pages	Thorat	2011	150.00
9789350238172	C Interviews Q&A, 2nd Edition 244 Pages	Thorat	2012	225.00
9788184046564	C++ for Beginners, 403 Pages	Harwani	2009	400.00
9789350231012	Core Java for Beginners, (B/CD), 892 Pages	Shah	2010	575.00
9788184046694	Database Concepts and Systems for Students, 3/ed, 428 Pgs	Bayross	2009	375.00
9789350239995	**E-Marketing for Beginners, 168 Pages**	**Gadkari**	**2013**	**250.00**
9788184047059	Hibernate 3 for Beginners - Covers Java Persistence API (B/CD), 680 Pages	Shah	2009	500.00
9788184048780	HTML for Beginners, 2nd Edition, 416 Pages	Aibara	2010	575.00
9789350236475	HTML5 for Beginners, 564 Pages	Aibara	2012	450.00
9788184045697	Java EE 5 for Beginners, Revised & Enlarged 2/ed (B/CD), 1,192 Pages	Bayross	2008	575.00
9788184049398	Java EE 6 for Beginners, (B/CD), 1092 Pages	Shah	2009	825.00
9788184049411	Java EE 6 Server Programming for Professionals (B/DVD), 1,328 Pages	Shah	2010	950.00
9788184048063	Java EE Project using EJB 3, JPA and Struts 2 for Beginners, (B/CD), 1258 Pages	Shah	2009	1,025.00
9789351103493	**Java EE 7 for Beginners, (B/CD), 1280 Pages**	**Shah**	**2013**	**1,300.00**
9789350237557	Java for Beginners, 2nd Edition (B/CD), Covers Java SE 7 JDK, 576 Pages	Chavan	2012	550.00
9788184045932	Java for Professionals: A Practical Approach to Java Programming (Covers Java SE 6), 790 Pages	Harwani	2008	525.00
9789350233719	Java for Students, 2nd Edition, 850 Pages	Phorwani	2011	600.00
9788184047097	Java Persistence API in EJB 3 for Professionals, (B/CD) 756 Pgs	Shah	2009	550.00
9788184043594	Java Server Pages for Beginners (B/CD), 872 Pages	Bayross	2007	500.00
9788184045925	Java Server Pages Project for Beginners, (B/CD), 746 Pages	Shah	2008	550.00
9788184048438	Lamp Programming for Professionals, (B/CD), 1,284	Shah	2009	975.00
9789350233986	Mobile Computing for Beginners, 782 Pages	Shende	2012	750.00
9788184040142	MySQL 5 for Professionals (B/CD), 770 Pages	Bayross	2005	550.00
9789350235188	MySQL 5.1 for professionals (B/CD), 772 Pages	Bayross	2011	650.00
9788184045260	Oracle for Professionals (Covers Oracle 9i, 10g & 11g) (B/CD), 1,420 Pgs	Shah	2008	975.00
9788184043228	PC Hardware for Beginners, 308 Pages	Sangia	2007	300.00
9788184040753	PHP 5.1 for Beginners (B/CD), 1,284 Pages	Bayross	2006	725.00
9788184048445	PHP Project for Beginners, (B/CD), 1,200 Pages	Shah	2011	600.00

ISBN	Title	Author	Year	Price
9788184047073	Practical ASP.NET 3.5 Projects for Beginners, (B/CD), 550 Pgs	Harwani	2009	450.00
9788184048070	Practical EJB Project for Beginners, 312 Pages	Harwani	2009	325.00
9788184043426	Practical Java Project for Beginners (B/CD), 164 Pages	Harwani	2007	175.00
9788184043419	Practical Web Services for Beginners, 168 Pages	Harwani	2007	150.00
9789350234907	Programming With PL/SQL for Beginners, 236 Pages	Patil	2011	300.00
9789350231241	QTP for Professionals, 480 Pages	Reddy	2010	450.00
9789350236499	SAP MM for Beginners, 384 Pages	Rakshit	2012	525.00
9789350233894	SAP SD for Beginners, 2/ed, 252 Pages	Samad	2011	350.00
9789350236482	Software Automation Testing Tools for Beginners, 1,112 Pages	Shende	2012	1,000.00
9789350231050	Software Documentation for Professionals, 600 Pages	Shah	2012	450.00
9789350236901	Spring 3 for Beginners (Book/CD-Rom), 612 Pages	Shah	2012	575.00
9789350237755	Spring 3 with Hibernate 4 Project for Professionals, (B/DVD), 886 Pages	Shah	2012	750.00
9788184047448	Struts 2 for Beginners, 2/ed, (B/CD), 566 Pages	Shah	2009	525.00
9788184046960	Struts 2 with Hibernate 3 Project for Beginners, (B/CD), 1,042 Pages	Shah	2009	775.00
9789350231043	**Struts 2 for Beginners, 3/Ed (B/Cd), 444 Pages**	**Shah**	**2013**	**600.00**
9788184041071	Visual Basic 2005 for Beginners (B/CD), 1,172 Pages	Bayross	2006	150.00
9789351102502	**Windows 8 with Office 2013 for Beginners, 786 Pages**	**Shah**	**2013**	**400.00**

Other Computer Titles

ISBN	Title	Author	Year	Price
9789350230237	A Primer on Software Quality Models & Project Management, 640 Pages	Mehta	2010	900.00
9788184048827	Art of Creative Destruction: Illustarted Software Testing & Test Automation....for the Testing Times, 2/ed, 248 Pages	Puranik	2010	425.00
9789350232859	Beginning Web Development for Smartphones Developing Web Applications with PHP, MySQL and jQTouch, 252 Pages	Harwani	2011	300.00
9789350237526	Business @ Cloud Level, 272 Pages	Yadav	2012	425.00
9789350231029	C# 4.0 Programming Made Easy, 624 Pages	Kadam	2011	425.00
9789350230244	Computer Architecture and Maintenance, 320 Pages	Kadam	2010	250.00
9789350235553	Data Structure and Algorithm, 492 Pages	Rukadikar	2011	400.00
9789351101154	**Excel - Vba For Managers, 292 Pages**	**Trehan**	**2013**	**600.00**
9788184048957	FAQ's in MFC and MFC Solutions, Vol I (B/CD), 510 Pages	P. G. Naik	2010	425.00
9788173666810	First Encounter with Java Including BlueJ, 386 Pages	Bhutta	2006	225.00
9789350230275	Instant Oracle, 100 Pages	Shah	2010	75.00
9788173664632	Introducing MySQL, 96 Pages	Oak	2005	50.00
9789350230251	Management Information System (MIS), 176 Pages	Kadam	2010	200.00
9789350231258	Maximum Oracle with Oracle Best Practices, 772 Pages	Puranik	2011	675.00
9788184043402	Operating Systems, 376 Pages	Sumitradevi	2008	300.00
9788184047899	Operating Systems, 2/ed, 408 Pages	Sumitradevi	2009	400.00
9789350234242	Oracle Financials 11i: A Practical Guide for the Beginners, 392 Pages	Peri	2011	725.00
9789350236918	Oracle Financials 11i, 2/ed: A Practical Guide for the Beginners, 436 Pages	Peri	2012	725.00
9789351101758	**Soft Computing, 224 Pages**	**Deva**	**2013**	**350.00**
9788173668012	Software Defect Prevention Concepts and Implementation, 180 Pages (H/B)	Kane & Bajaj	2003	300.00
9789350236307	Software Testing: Interview Questions, 176 Pages	Reddy	2012	175.00
9788173668814	Strategic Bidding: A Successful Approach (for IT / Consultancy), 192 Pgs	Garg	2004	275.00
9789350237120	**Testing in 30+ Open Source Tools, 2nd Edition, (B/CD), 1,340 Pages**	**Shende**	**2013**	**975.00**
9788173660429	Vijay Mukhi's ERP Odyssey: Implementing People Soft Financials 7.0/7.5, 528 Pages	Mukhi	1999	350.00

Business, Management & Finance

ISBN	Title	Author	Year	Price
9789350238936	100% Forex Learning and Earning (Natural Shade Paper Use) 236 Pages	Darazhanov	2012	275.00
9788184046977	An Introduction to Foreign Exchange & Financial Risk Management, (B/CD), 348 Pages	Lakshman	2009	400.00

ISBN	Title	Author	Year	Price
9789350230268	Bootstrapping A Software Company, 348 Pages	Yadav	2010	425.00
9788184044249	Break Your Negative Attitude, 114 Pages	Dr. Mishra	2007	125.00
9788184040425	Developing Analytical Skills: Case Studies in Management, 636 Pages	Dr. Natarajan	2008	500.00
9788173660993	Doing Business with the French, 150 Pages	Jhangiani	1999	150.00
9788184044959	Enabling Event-ful Experiences, 250 Pages	Balachandran	2008	200.00
9789351102182	**Entrepreneurship Management, 192 Pages**	**Sharma**	**2013**	**200.00**
9789350237380	Ethical Supply Chain Management in India, 124 Pages	Fernandes	2012	200.00
9788184044744	Ethics, Indian Ethos and Management, 2nd/Ed 252 Pages	Balachandran	2008	175.00
9789350231227	Financial Decision Modeling Operations Research & Business Statistics, 696 Pages	Sridhar	2010	350.00
9789350238929	Financial Management: Problems & Solutions, 5/ed, 1,228 Pgs	Sridhar	2012	950.00
9789350237540	Fixed Income Markets in India: Investment Opportunities for You, 280 Pgs	Sen	2012	350.00
9789350239728	**Fixed Income Markets in India: Investment Opportunities for You, (2 Colour) 280 Pages**	**Apte**	**2013**	**750.00**
9789350231227	Financial Decision Modeling Operations Research & Business Statistics, 696 Pages	Sridhar	2010	350.00
9789350232965	Futures & Options: Equities-Trading Strategies & Skills, 4/ed, 392 Pages	Sridhar	2011	475.00
9789350233917	Globally Distributed Work, 276 Pages	Mehta	2011	425.00
9789350233887	Hospitality Management, 476 Pages	Shirke	2011	525.00
9788184040432	How to Eat The Elephant? The CEO's Guide To An Enterprise Sys Implementation, 104 Pages	Tulsyan	2007	325.00
9789350233108	How to Learn Management from your wife (HB), 96 Pages	Rangnekar	2011	275.00
9789350230459	How to Learn Management from your wife (PB), 96 Pages	Rangnekar	2010	125.00
9789350238097	**International Financial System & Institutions, 304 Pages**	**Arora**	**2013**	**400.00**
9789351103066	**Kuruvamma'S Saree "A Story Of Small Loans, Big Hopes", 120 Pgs**	**Ranjani**	**2013**	**200.00**
9788184044164	Logistics in International Business, 2/ed, 428 Pages	Aserkar	2007	450.00
9788184047547	Magic and Logic of Elliott Waves, The, 204 Pages	Kale	2009	500.00
9788184048568	Management Accounting & Financial Analysis for C.A.Final (June 2009), 9/ed, 540 Pages	Sridhar	2009	400.00
9789351100539	**Management Dynamics and Indian Ethos, 364 Pages**	**Mohan**	**2013**	**550.00**
9789350235126	Management of Services, 348 Pages	Poddar	2011	450.00
9789351102489	**Mutual Funds in India: Vehicle for Fixed Income Investments, 272 Pages**	**Sen**	**2013**	**400.00**
9788184047066	Purchasing and Inventory Management, 338 Pages	Menon	2009	475.00
9789350233870	Quantitative Techniques for Project Management, 268 Pages	Velayoudam	2011	600.00
9788173666797	Rules of Origin in International Trade, 238 Pages	Dr. Sathpathy	2005	300.00
9789350233580	Services Marketing, 448 Pages	Balachandran	2011	425.00
9789351101642	**Service Tax Guide For Professionals & Students, 324 Pgs**	**Knowledge Exchange**	**2013**	**450.00**
9789350233115	Soft Skills In Management, 148 Pages	Rangnekar	2011	175.00
9789351100461	**Spirituality At Workplace, 580 Pages**	**Svkm**	**2013**	**900.00**
9788173668814	Strategic Bidding: A Successful Approach (for IT / Consultancy), 192 Pages	Garg	2004	275.00
9789351103790	**Strategic Financial Management for C.A. Final, 12/ed (Nov 2013 Paper Solved) 818 Pages**	**Sridhar**	**2013**	**695.00**
9789350239438	Strategies For Improving Your Business Communication, 196 Pages	Rao	2012	250.00
9788184043211	Time Your Trades With Technical Analysis (B/CD), 348 Pages	Pradhan	2007	600.00
9789351101550	**Value Based Innovative Business Management, 716 Pages**	**Iqbal**	**2013**	**990.00**
9789350238127	Value Investing And Behavioral Finance, 180 Pages	Bhatt	2012	250.00
9789351101185	**Why Greed Is Great!!! Time To Create Your Money - Life Balance, 122 Pgs**	**Sen**	**2013**	**250.00**

ISBN	Title	Author	Year	Price
Catering & Hotel Management				
9788173668739	Careers in Hospitality - Hotel Management Entrance Exam Guide, 332 Pgs	Rego	2004	200.00
9789350238103	**Food and Beverage Management, 524 Pages**	**Shirke**	**2013**	**700.00**
9789350239537	**Food Production and Culinary Art, 524 Pages**	**Verma**	**2013**	**700.00**
9789350233887	Hospitality Management, 476 Pages	Shirke	2011	525.00
9789351101765	**Marvels of Indian Breakfast, 164 Pages**	**Shankaran**	**2013**	**250.00**
9789350238158	Marvels of Indian Jam, Juice, Sauce, Salad &....., 190 Pages	Shankaran	2012	250.00
9789350238141	Marvels of Indian Pickles, Chutneys and Condiments, 124 Pages	Shankaran	2012	200.00
9789350230817	Marvels of Indian Snacks, 264 Pages	Shankaran	2011	350.00
9789350238189	Marvels of Indian Sweets, 152 Pages	Shankaran	2012	250.00
9788184046687	Marvels of North Indian Cuisine, 196 Pages	Shankaran	2009	325.00
9788184044751	Marvels of South Indian Cuisine, 220 Pages	Shankaran	2008	250.00
9789351100638	**Wine And More, 260 Pages**	**Khanna**	**2013**	**750.00**
Civil Engineering				
9789350233252	Concrete for High Performance Sustainable Infrastructure, 312 Pages	Dhir	2011	750.00
9789350233245	New Developments in Concrete Construction, 296 Pages	Dhir	2011	750.00
9788184043785	Raina's Concrete Bridge Practice, 3/ed : Analysis, Design & Economics, 856 Pages	Dr. Raina	2007	TBA
9788184048056	Raina's Concrete Bridge Practice: Construction, Maintenance and Rehabiliation 2/ed, 452 Pages (H/B) [14 Full Color Inserts]	Dr. Raina	2010	625.00
9788184048049	Raina's Concrete Bridge: Inspection, Repair, Strengthening, Testing, Load Capacity Evaluation 2/ed, 800 Pages (H/B) [32 Full Color Inserts]	Dr. Raina	2010	800.00
9788184047530	Raina's Concrete for Construction: Facts and Practice, 400 Pages (H/B)	Dr. Raina	2009	650.00
9788184047875	Raina's Construction & Contract Management, 2/ed Inside Story, 585 Pages (H/B)	Dr. Raina	2009	850.00
9788184046618	Raina's Field Manual for Highway and Bridge Engineers, 3/ed, 1,404 Pgs	Dr. Raina	2009	1,800.00
9789350231418	Raina's Handbook For Concrete Bridges, (Set of 2 Volumes), 2088 Pgs	Dr. Raina	2012	8,000.00
9788184040135	The World of Bridges, 300 Pages (H/B) [4 color]	Dr. Raina	2006	1,000.00
9789350231180	Using Primavera 6: Planning, Executing, Monitoring and Controlling Projects, 228 Pages	Al-Saridi	2010	350.00
Communication				
9788184047905	Enhancing Soft Skills, 346 Pages	Biswas	2009	400.00
9789350231265	Knowing Your Words Worth: A Practical Guide to Communicating Effectively in English, 180 Pages	Shirodkar	2011	225.00
9789350239438	Strategies For Improving Your Business Communication, 196 Pages	Rao	2012	250.00
9789351101444	**Unscrambling Emails The Knowing Your Words Worth Series, 144 Pages**	**Shirodkar**	**2013**	**200.00**
Dental / Health / Medical				
9789351100027	**Cancer: A Comma, not a Fullstop, 196 Pages**	**Venkatesh**	**2013**	**275.00**
9789351100485	**My Family Doctor, 176 Pages**	**Dr. Gadkari**	**2013**	**200.00**
9788173660986	Notes on Pathology, 11th Millennium Edition, 482 Pages	Experienced Prof.	2000	350.00
9788173668975	Splinting Management of MOBILE & Migrating Teeth, 104 Pgs	Dr. Kakar	2004	150.00
9788173669798	The Balancing Act "A Win Over Obesity", 296 Pages	Dr. Gadkari	2005	225.00
9788184049480	The Balancing Act "Know Your Heart", 368 Pages	Dr. Gadkari	2010	325.00
Economics				
9788184043266	Analysing Macroeconomics: A Toolkit for Managers, Executives & Students (Hardback), 156 Pages	Rakesh Singh	2007	500.00

ISBN	Title	Author	Year	Price
9788184044171	Analysing Macroeconomics: A Toolkit for Managers, Executives & Students (Paperback), 156 Pages	Rakesh Singh	2007	250.00
9788173666797	Rules of Origin in International Trade, 238 Pages	Dr. Sathpathy	2005	300.00
Education				
9789350239674	**Academic Excellence, 236 Pages**	**Shetty**	**2013**	**300.00**
9789351100102	**Funding Techniques of World Renowned Universities, 204 Pages**	**Dharaskar**	**2013**	**500.00**
9789351102281	**Strategy To Develop World Class University, 508 Pages**	**Dharaskar**	**2013**	**650.00**
9789351103080	**Technology-Storms Redefining World Class Universities, 416 Pgs**	**Dharaskar**	**2013**	**800.00**
Electrical Engineering				
9788184043235	Basic Electrical Circuits, 2/ed, 368 Pages	Dr. Salam	2007	250.00
Electronics & Communication				
9788173669002	Electronic Components and Materials, 3/ed, 404 Pages	Joshi	2004	175.00
Electronics & Engineering				
9788173660772	Principles of Environmental Science Engineering and Maintenance, 288 Pages	Dr. Thirumurthy	2004	175.00
Engineering & Science				
9789350239681	**MATLAB® Programming for Engineering and Science, 204 Pages**	**Dey**	**2013**	**375.00**
9789350237199	**Understanding Matlab, 390 Pages**	**Manza**	**2013**	**450.00**
Event Management				
9788184044959	Enabling Event-ful Experiences, 250 Pages	Balachandran	2008	250.00
General Titles				
9788184045642	Hello Police Station (Marathi), 118 Pages	Shinde	2008	100.00
9789351102175	**Jars Filled With Gold, 252 Pages**	**Malshe**	**2013**	**350.00**
9789351103134	**Nixie The Mermaid and The Power of Love, 204 Pages**	**Suryavanshi**	**2013**	**250.00**
9789350236338	Residential Interior Design for the Elderly and Physically Challenged, 200 Pgs	Ray	2012	450.00
HRD				
9788184047080	Departmental Enquiries: Concept, Procedure & Practice, 534 Pages	Goel	2009	475.00
9788184040425	Developing Analytical Skills: Case Studies in Management, 636 Pgs	Dr. Natarajan	2008	500.00
9788184044744	Ethics, Indian Ethos and Management, 2nd/Ed 252 Pages	Balachandran	2008	175.00
9788184046229	How To Improve Trainer Effectiveness, 170 Pages	Balachandran	2008	200.00
International Trade				
9789350239124	**Regional Trade Agreements, 320 Pages**	**Kamat**	**2013**	**750.00**
Law				
9789350230800	A Handbook on the Maintenance & Welfare of Parents and Senior Citizens Act, 2007., 160 Pages	Gracias	2010	150.00
9788173664161	Customs Valuation in India 3/ed, 262 Pages	Satapathy	2002	375.00
9789351103073	**Global Business Laws & Taxation, 456 Pages**	**Iqbal**	**2013**	**650.00**
9788173661426	Law of Sale of Goods & Partnership, 228 Pages	Chandiramani	2000	150.00
9788184042481	Laws of Carriage of Goods By Sea & Multimodal Transport In India, 92 Pages	Hariharan	2007	60.00
9788173666797	Rules of Origin in International Trade, 238 Pages	Dr. Sathpathy	2005	300.00
9789350231289	Social Security, Insurance and the Law, 460 Pages	Gopalakrishna	2011	600.00

ISBN	Title	Author	Year	Price
Learning Disability				
9789350233924	On the wave of Brain: A Broad Perspective of Learning Disability 300 Pages	Jain	2011	450.00
Marine				
9788184043242	Containerisation, Multimodal Transport and Infrastructure Development in India, 5/ed, 852 Pages	Hariharan	2007	650.00
9788173665516	A Textbook on Container & Multimodal Transport Management, 522 Pgs	Dr. Hariharan	2002	600.00
9788184043242	Containerisation, Multimodal Transport and Infrastructure Development in India, 5/ed, 852 Pages	Hariharan	2007	650.00
9788184043136	Marine Control Technology, 336 Pages	Majumder	2007	425.00
9788173669279	Marine Diesel Engines, 428 Pages	Aranha	2004	250.00
9789350238905	**Marine Electrical Technology, 6/ed, 1,180 Pages**	**Fernandes**	**2013**	**950.00**
9788173660801	Marine Internal Combustion Engines, 272 Pages	Kane	2003	275.00
9788173661419	Maritime Education, Training & Assessment Manual (TAP) - Vol II, 474 Pages,	DG Shipping	1999	400.00
9788173660375	Merchant Shipping: (STCW) Rules, 1998 incl. Training & Assessment Programme - 1,216 Pages	DG Shipping	1998	225.00
Mathematics				
9789350236796	Graph Theory with Applications, 812 Pages	Dey	2012	300.00
Mechanical Engineering				
9789350236192	Glance On Transformer Oil, A 96 Pages	Pandey	2012	125.00
9789351102168	**A Glance On Three Phase Squirrel Gage Induction Motor, 172 Pages**	**Pandey**	**2013**	**225.00**
Media				
9789351100249	**Media Madness & The Awesome 3 Some - Main Anjaani, 156 Pages**	**Kapoor**	**2013**	**175.00**
Mobile Computing				
9789350232859	Beginning Web Development for Smartphones Developing Web Applications with PHP, MySQL and JqTouch, 252 Pages	Harwani	2011	300.00
9789350233986	Mobile Computing for Beginners, 1,059 Pages	Shende	2012	750.00
Motivation / Self Help				
9788184044249	Break Your Negative Attitude, 114 Pages	Dr. Mishra	2007	125.00
9788184047905	Enhancing Soft Skills, 346 Pages	Biswas	2009	400.00
9788173665271	Heads You Win, Tails You Win, 2/ed, 200 Pages	Dr.Mishra	2005	200.00
9789351101062	**I am A Miracle Being, 50 Pages**	**Awatramani**	**2013**	**149.00**
9789350236208	Life is Fundamentally Management!, 200 Pages	Senthival	2012	250.00
9789350230206	Nothing Is Absolute, 274 Pages	Balachandran	2010	300.00
9789350237113	Secrets of Your Leadership Success: The 11 Indispensable E's of a Leader, 212 Pages	Rao	2012	350.00
9789350238165	Sharpen Your Mind, 242 Pages	Rao	2012	350.00
9789350238080	Skills for your Career Success: Touch your Tipping Point, 135 Pages	Sai	2012	175.00
9789350237533	Smart Moves Great Career, 148 Pages	Rastogi	2012	150.00
9789351101635	**Student Leaders: Growing From Students to Ceos, 296 Pages**	**Rao**	**2013**	**300.00**
9789351102496	**Success Tools For Ceo Coaches Be A Learner, Leader, And Ladder, 244 Pages**	**Rao**	**2013**	**350.00**
9789350238134	White Magique, 124 Pages	Herekar	2012	200.00

ISBN	Title	Author	Year	Price
Parenting				
9789350231760	Mom Don't Spoil Me, 140 Pages	Dr. C. S. Mishra	2010	150.00
Project Management / Software Engineering				
9789350230237	A Primer on Software Quality Models & Project Management, 640 Pages	Mehta	2010	900.00
9789350233870	Quantitative Techniques for Project Management, 268 Pages	Velayoudam	2011	600.00
Science				
9788184043259	Gravitation Demythicised: An Introduction to Einstein's General Relativity and Cosmology for Common Man, 258 Pages	Shenoy	2007	250.00
9789351101499	**Fundamentals Of Botany (First Year B.Sc.), 344 Pages**	**Vaidya**	**2013**	**300.00**
9788184047912	Theoretical Physics - Volume I: Relativistic Theory and Electrodynamics, 490 Pages	Prof Fai	2010	650.00
9788184047929	Study Aid Theoretical Physics - Volume I: Relativistic Theory and Electrodynamics, 418 Pgs	Prof Fai	2010	475.00

- **All Prices are in Indian Rupees**
- **Titles Released after January 2013 are marked in Bold.**